Torn and Frayed

TORN AND FRAYED

*Congressional Norms and Party Switching
in an Era of Reform*

Judd Choate

Westport, Connecticut
London

Library of Congress Cataloging-in-Publication Data

Choate, Judd, 1969–
    Torn and frayed : congressional norms and party switching in an era of reform / Judd
Choate.
        p. cm.
    Includes bibliographical references (p.) and index.
    ISBN 0–275–97790–0 (alk. paper)
        1. United States. Congress. House.   2. Legislators—United States.   3. Party
    affiliation—United States.   I. Title.
    JK1319C46   2003
    328.73′0769—dc21   2002037060

British Library Cataloguing in Publication Data is available.

Library of Congress Catalog Card Number: 2002037060
ISBN: 0–275–97790–0

First published in 2003

Praeger Publishers, 88 Post Road West, Westport, CT 06881
An imprint of Greenwood Publishing Group, Inc.
www.praeger.com

Printed in the United States of America

The paper used in this book complies with the
Permanent Paper Standard issued by the National
Information Standards Organization (Z39.48–1984).

10   9   8   7   6   5   4   3   2   1

To Dad

CONTENTS

ACKNOWLEDGMENTS

Although I could not possibly have known it at the time, I began work on this book in Barbara Hinckley's political behavior research seminar at Purdue University, the fall of 1994. We were required to design and carry out a research project to be completed by the end of the semester. I made the now unfathomable choice to test at the state level the central thesis in Barbara's first book, *The Seniority System in Congress*. In a paper that makes me cringe in embarrassment, I concluded that the seniority system was dead in the Indiana House of Representatives, a conclusion that was overly simplistic and has since been proven wholly incorrect. Instead of being put off that a 24-year-old graduate student would dare challenge her findings, Barbara was sincerely excited that I would show interest in a subject she felt had been abandoned by congressional scholars after the Sunshine reforms. Over the next year and a half, Barbara spent hours helping me draft and redraft early versions of what would ultimately become *Torn and Frayed*.

This book goes against the discipline's prevailing methodological current. It is not the product of a formal model, nor does it arise from a previously collected dataset. Instead, it is theory-driven research. Barbara made sure of that. She insisted that I devise and test my own theories, collect my own data, and avoid the trampled down path of the road too much traveled in our discipline. For that, and so many other pearls of wisdom, I owe my unending gratitude to Barbara—not so much for her ideas on this particular project, but for her insistence that I trust my instincts and find my own way. Sadly, Barbara did not live to read even the first draft, but that makes her contribution no less important. She was an incredibly supportive adviser, mentor, and friend throughout my career, and her advice still guides me to this day.

In the end, I cannot help but be proud of this book, not so much for the quality of the final product but for the fact that it was drafted during the most difficult period of my life. And, if it is true that what doesn't kill you makes you stronger, then I am a much stronger person today thanks in no small part to a number friends and colleagues who assisted me during this period. I would like to take this opportunity to thank them.

I wish to thank Robert X Browning, who was remarkably charitable with his time during the drafting of this book. He was always ready with a red pen whenever one was necessary. Other very supportive friends in the academic world include Eric Waltenburg, Rosalee Clawson, Silvo Lenart, Cindy Weber, Pat Boling, Keith Shimko, Will Heller, Brian Humes, and John Gruhl.

The member interviews are the central feature of the research, thus, I owe a great debt to the members who participated: Thomas Bliley (R-VA); David Bonior (D-MI); Sam Brownback (R-KS); Dan Burton (R-IN); Steve Buyer (R-IN); Bob Clement (D-TN); Tom Coburn (R-OK); Nathan Deal (R-GA); Lee Hamilton (D-IN); Scott Klug (R-WI); Greg Laughlin (R-TX); Bob Livingston (R-LA); Jan Meyers (R-KS); Carlos Moorhead (R-CA); John Myers (R-IN); David Obey (D-WI); Michael Oxley (R-OH); Mike Parker (R-MS); Pat Roberts (R-KS); Tim Roemer (D-IN); Bernard Sanders (I-VT); Billy Tauzin (R-LA); Todd Tiahrt (R-KS). Jan Meyers, Greg Laughlin, Pat Roberts, and Bob Livingston were especially giving of their time. These came as a result of numerous helpful staffers who squeezed me in despite scheduling difficulties and contrasting priorities.

A big thank you goes out to everyone at Praeger for their assistance in this process, especially my editor. Michael Hermann has been everything an editor should be, supportive and encouraging, forceful but understanding. It has been a pleasure working with him ... All Down the Line. I also thank the reviewers for their thoughtful comments, which were both validating and demanding. The manuscript is much better now in no small part because of the time and dedication my reviewers put into their important role.

In addition to my formal advisers and research participants, I want to take this opportunity to thank the one person without whose help I could not possibly have completed this book. Lyn Kathlene is much more than my partner, she is my conscience and my advocate. She helps me see the world as it is without losing sight of what it can be. With Lyn, it was never a question of whether I would finish *Torn and Frayed,* only a question of when. For these reasons and so many more, I cannot possibly thank you enough Lyn.

Before I even knew that congressional norms existed, I was already indebted to Larry Gould, my first academic adviser and current Provost at Fort Hays State University in Hays, Kansas. More than anyone I know, Larry pays it forward. Keep asking Larry, I will say "yes" someday.

I am indebted to a number of friends who helped me substantively or otherwise over the years, most notably Chris Sook, who has been my best friend for two-thirds of my life. Chris patiently listens to my diatribes, laughs at my jokes, and joins me in agonizing over the Royals each season. He's the brother I always longed for.

Other supportive friends and family members include Elizabeth Neeley, Alan Tomkins, Karen Reynolds, Kari O'Neill, Ramzi Dewing and everyone at the University of Nebraska Public Policy Center, Jane Schoenike, Jean McNeil and everyone at the Nebraska State Bar Association, Justice John Gerrard, Dan Harris, Judy Beutler and the other members of the minority and Justice Task Force, Jewlya Lynn, David Wallick, Mahlon "Mae" Wallick, Jeanne Allen, and Lorrie Hill, Johnna Shackelford, A.J. Kirkpatrick, Matt Rhea, David Reigle, Brent Coup, Melissa Bolig, and Brenda Kasper. Some four-legged family members, here and gone, who have made my life so much richer are Chami, Princess, Sara Chamois, Knox, Darwin, Abby, Rocky, Chili, Sunshine, Pirate, and Ida B. Wells.

I also would like to thank my grandparents. I come from a very small, close-knit family where every relationship is important. I have been amazingly fortunate to grow into adulthood under the watchful eye of the four most wonderful grandparents a person could possibly have. We recently lost Woody and, as I write this, my other grandfather, Joe, is in very poor health, but the effect that each of my grandparents have had and continue to have on my life will far outlive them. Alyce, Woody, June, and Joe were and are wonderful people, who by an accident of genetics, I am lucky enough to call my family.

Finally, I thank my parents, Jerry and Fi Choate, whose love and guidance have been a constant in my life. They are my closest friends and my trusted confidants. I love them more than I can express in words. Everything positive I am today is directly a consequence of my mom's wisdom and my dad's temperament. All negative traits are mine and mine alone.

Six years ago, I dedicated my Ph.D. dissertation to my mom. *Torn and Frayed* I dedicate to my dad.

Chapter 1

AN EXAMINATION OF CONGRESSIONAL NORMS

When Vermont Senator Jim Jeffords left the Republican Party in May of 2001, to become an independent that votes with the Democratic Party, he shifted legislative power from the Republican Party to the Democratic Party and ended the first 50–50 split in the history of the U.S. Senate. But why would he take such an action? House members and senators switch parties for one or a combination of three reasons: party realignment in their home state, professional gain, or personal gain. In Jeffords' case, while one of the most liberal states in the country, Vermont re-elected Jeffords seven months earlier with 66 percent of the vote. So, it is safe to say that his seat was not in jeopardy. As a senior Republican in his third term, he gains little professionally from the switch, and could potentially damage relationships with important members on both sides of the aisle. Thus, it seems likely that Jeffords made the switch for personal reasons, perhaps linked to ideology. This is highly unusual in the U.S. Congress and violates an important "norm" of congressional behavior, namely that you "dance with who brung you."

Jeffords' situation is unusual and created some difficult decisions for the Democratic Party. Rarely are members or senators so offended by their colleagues or the president as to seek such a radical remedy. In fact, for most members there is little utility in violating the informal rule regarding party cohesiveness. Elected officials understand that they cannot survive without their party and their party cannot survive without them, so senators and House members alike attempt to identify themselves through their actions and votes as a member of a political party. The party then rewards members with plum committee or leadership posts, based, at least partially, on consistent loyalty to the party. This consistency or "predictability" is fundamental to the life of the institution and has outlived institutional reforms, party alignments, and leadership upheaval. While Congress operates by a series of formalized rules of congressional action and member behavior, the informal rules are what govern the institution.

NORMS OF CONGRESS

The three norms of seniority, specialization, and reciprocity have been, and continue to be, fundamental to the congressional committee system. A member's length of tenure, area of expertise, and persuasive skills establish his or her influence and prestige within and, to some extent, outside the institution. In short, congressional norms help to establish an informal "pecking order" based on duration of service and issue expertise that permeates the policy-making process and provides stability for both the members and the institution.

Two forces led to the growth and adoption of congressional norms. First, the nature of the institution fosters the desire for consistency and predictability, those attributes most closely associated with congressional norms (Polsby, Gallaher, and Rundquist 1971; Rohde, Ornstein, and Peabody 1985). Moreover, norms were embraced to further the individual and professional interests of the members (Hinckley 1976; Weingast 1979; Hinckley 1988). Membership evolves however, and so do member attitudes and interests. Thus, from time to time, the institution becomes less stable. During these periods, reforms are adopted that can threaten the informal rules. Despite these periods of relative instability, however, institutional norms adapt and survive because they originally were adopted by the institution to further the goals of the members. Thus, unless member goals change, the norms will be retained in one form or another, and to this point, there is little evidence of changing member goals.

This book examines the informal rules of the U.S. House of Representatives. This was once a principal area of congressional research. Several of the discipline's most prominent scholars authored important books and articles chronicling the history of and prospects for congressional norms (Matthews 1960; Polsby, Gallaher, and Rundquist 1969; Fenno 1971; Polsby 1971; Hinckley 1971; Asher 1973; Matthews and Stimson 1975; Hinckley 1976). Since the 1970s, however, most scholarship has steered away from norms, focusing instead on election dynamics, roll call votes, and interest group scores, with only occasional research concerning seniority rule violations or committee chair battles.

The 1970s proved to be an era of arresting reform in the House, much of which directly or indirectly affected the seniority, specialization, and reciprocity norms. Interestingly, however, articles and book chapters from several prominent researchers suggest that this period illustrates the *stability* of most institutional features, including congressional norms and not the fragility of said norms (Rieselbach 1978; Polsby 1983; Sinclair 1983; Rohde, Ornstein, and Peabody 1985; Hinckley 1988; Rieselbach 1994; Thurber and Davidson 1995). As Rohde et al. put it, "[Congress] has changed in many ways since the 1950s. Yet perhaps the most striking thing . . . is the continuity of [its] folkways" (1973, 179).

Norm research has focused on committee practices, the Sunshine reforms of the 1970s, and the apprenticeship of younger members. Unfortunately, these research topics have not engendered interaction with actual members to determine their evolving attitudes toward these norms. Consequently, students of Congress have only the most limited understanding of the attitudinal differences that exist between and among members and the effects these differences have on a changing institution. The project that follows helps to explain the intense desire for reform that accompanies high congressional turnover found by other researchers (Hinckley 1976; Rieselbach 1994; Thurber and Davidson 1995; Aldrich and Rohde 1997). It also helps to explain why more senior members are reluctant to reform the informal rules of congress while younger, less tenured members find reform more appealing. Furthermore, since some congressional scholars, Rohde (1988), Smith (1989), Moore and Herrick (1993), argue that norms are less important since what Polsby termed "the highly cohesive, bounded institutions of the 1950s and 1960s," a relationship can be inferred between House institutionalization and norm adherence (Polsby 1968, 93). In short, an understanding of member attitudes toward congressional norms helps to explain committee processes, member interaction dynamics, institutional resistance, member turnover, party switching, and a host of other questions.

The first, and perhaps most instructive consequence of an examination of member attitudes toward norms, is a greater understanding of House institutionalization, where the informal "folkways" are engrained in its members. An "institutionalized" organization refers to the likelihood that its members will act predictably in accordance with tradition. In the case of the U.S. House, it was a highly institutionalized chamber prior to 1971, but underwent a series of reforms in the decade that altered the impermeability of its folkways. In the 1980s, however, the House once

again became a predictable institution that asserted its traditional hierarchy based on tenure and adherence to rules. The 1994 election of 87
new freshman Republicans saw yet another reversal. The new House
Republican leadership ushered in numerous reforms and institutional
changes that have further eroded the informal powers of committee leaders, in addition to limiting the tenure of committee chairs (Deering and
Smith 1997).

The data examined here seeks to illustrate the connection between
institutionalism and norm adherence and posits the future for norms in
a less institutionalized House. To the outside world, the election of a
new majority party or individual members changing parties may seem
chaotic. In reality, however, even the most disruptive member actions
are managed through application of basic institutional norms. Moreover,
this book examines three specific challenges facing congressional norms,
as well as the effects these challenges are having and will continue to
have on the institution's folkways. Finally, the members themselves discuss the positives and negatives of the three norms so closely identified
with committee work, seniority, specialization, and reciprocity. In short,
member responses demonstrate the reason that congressional norms remain: the members believe they are important. These findings demonstrate
the resiliency of the institutional norms, despite times of anti-establishment
sentiment.

This is not simply an examination of member turnover or congressional norms however. Instead, it is an examination of the stability of
the U.S. House, and specifically, the stability of membership attitudes
and the adoption of congressional norms as fundamental to the successful
operation of the U.S. House of Representatives. Since the 1960s, seniority, specialization, and reciprocity have been relaxed to meet the
changing membership or attitudes of the day, but they have not been
abandoned. Members come and go, reforms are attempted and abandoned, but the norms adapt and survive.

DEFINING NORMS

The formal rules of the House are those written, debated, and adopted
by the House at the beginning of each congressional session (Oleszek
1996). They include rules governing parliamentary procedures, bill introduction, debate, and passage, committee jurisdiction, and lobbying
restrictions, among others. It is not uncommon that a shift in membership
produces rule reform, but this reform rarely affects the underlying principle of the norm. For instance, the large turnover in the Democratic

Party beginning in 1971 and culminating in 1975 brought about several rule changes that fragmented House interests and empowered its membership (Davidson, 1992; Rieselbach 1994). Another membership turnover in 1992 and 1994 promoted a different set of reforms (Koopman 1996; Aldrich and Rohde 1997; Deering and Smith 1997), which might appear similar but in practice have a much different effect, as will be discussed in later chapters.

The informal rules of the institution are unwritten but no less important, for they demand member adherence to tradition, traditions that guide member behavior and have done so for hundreds of years. Sociologists define norms as "standards of human conduct accepted in a given situation at a given time" (Birenbaum and Sagarin 1976, 6). These can be as simple as a typical letter salutation and as complicated as table manners at Buckingham Palace, but in either case they impart a prescribed course of action in the given situation.

Norms are adopted to promote interests. In a large and diverse group, they are often adopted to further the interests of a majority of group members. Weingast argues that norms are a situational construct that evolves over an extended time period (1979). This appears to be the case in the U.S. Congress, where the norms have been codified by several generations of legislators who advocated consistent, predictable behavior from the leadership as well as from other members. Each of the three major norms and the dozens of minor norms discussed here advantage a majority of individual members and/or the institution, hence their adoption and continued importance.

This extends beyond individual action to groups as well. All organizations, communities, and institutions live by a set of social standards that serve to normalize interactions by creating an implied social hierarchy. Norms are designed to simplify the choices and impart rationality by enumerating available alternatives in a given situation. In a sense, a norm describes the type of behavior prescribed by most, if not all members of the group and often, though not always, produces sanctions for deviance. Conversely, those who most closely adhere to the norms "are likely to emerge as . . . leaders and form what is often called an 'Establishment'" (Birenbaum and Sagarin 1976, 6). As with the formal rules, however, the informal rules can also be reformed. Based on the evidence from several periods of congressional history, it appears that membership turnover promotes this type of change as well (Hinckley 1976; Hinckley 1988; Deering and Smith 1997).

The two House reform periods of the last 25 years have brought about a relaxation of several congressional norms. Why has this occurred? Not all members support the major House norms. Younger, less tenured members are more resistant to norms because their predictability helps to establish a hierarchy of power (which finds the freshman members at the bottom), and they aid the establishment when the younger member likely won election by criticizing or even defeating an establishment candidate. Thus, periods of great turnover mean large numbers of new members, and large numbers of new members mean a much greater likelihood of institutional reform and a relaxation of the norms. That said, despite the Sunshine reforms (1971–75) and the Contract with America reforms (1995), seniority is still the first determinant of committee leadership selection, specialization still promotes individual member influence within and outside the chamber, and cooperative arrangements between members are still advocated as a way to further this influence. Thus, reforms threaten norms, but rarely do they eliminate norms.

NORM IMPORTANCE

Although other scholars investigated the importance of traditional practices in the House prior to 1960, Donald Matthews was the first to fully describe congressional norms and their use in his groundbreaking book *U.S. Senators and Their World* (1960). Using primarily anecdotal data, Matthews argues that the Senate is governed by the informal relationships arising from institutional norms. Specifically, he found the existence of several norms including: apprenticeship, legislative work, specialization, courtesy, reciprocity, and institutional patriotism. Subsequent analytic studies of the U.S. House indicate the existence of similar relationship dynamics in the House as well (Clark 1963; Fenno 1965; Polsby 1968; Matthews and Stimson 1975).

Of the norms described by Matthews, three, apprenticeship, specialization, and reciprocity, are directly tied to the committee system. It is widely argued, however, that the apprenticeship norm no longer exists, at least not in the form it once did, leaving two of Matthews' committee-based norms (Hinckley 1988; Smith 1989, Moore and Herrick 1993, Uslaner 1993). Subsequent scholarship proposed the existence of a seniority norm and its by-product the seniority rule, the practice of selecting the most senior majority party committee member as committee chair. Seniority, specialization, and reciprocity were selected for this analysis because they serve to define the committee system of an institutionalized House. Thus, researching them not only provides insights into member attitudes toward institution traditions, it also demonstrates the member attitudes toward the committee system as well.

Following the early norm research by Matthews and others (Polsby, Gallaher, and Rundquist 1969; Fenno 1971; Polsby 1971; Hinckley 1971; Asher 1973), the membership turnover that spawned the reform period of the early 1970s weakened congressional norms. Over the 92d, 93rd, and 94th Congresses, the Democratic majority, dominated by young reformists, relaxed the seniority rule and adopted the Sunshine reforms, which opened up the committee system by shifting policy making influence from committees to subcommittees (Rieselbach 1978; Rohde and Shepsle 1978; Price 1978; Rohde 1991; Rieselbach 1994; Thurber and Davidson 1995). In addition to reforming the committee and subcommittee chair selection process, the Sunshine reforms relaxed the need for member specialization and reciprocity as members sidestepped the committee process and took amendments straight to House floor (Smith 1986; Smith 1989). Thus, the membership turnover that brought about formal institutional change also promoted informal institutional change, both directly, through seniority system reforms, and indirectly, through committee and subcommittee reforms.

Barbara Hinckley examined this idea in "Seniority 1975: Old Theories Confront New Facts," researching the effect these reforms had on the seniority system and institutional stability as a whole (1976). She argues that the reforms of the 1970s were a localized event caused by the confluence of factors, most notably a sharp increase in junior legislators. This assessment is based in the belief that norms are adaptive and resilient, even in times of institutional change. History supports Hinckley's claim. Following three committee chairmanship violations in 1975 alone, only one more violation occurred in the next 20 years. The factors necessary to bring about more violations only resurfaced in abundance following the 1994 congressional elections, prompting another three violations.

In addition to the research on the U.S. Congress, studies have found that norms exist outside of the U.S. legislative system as well (Kornberg 1964; Crowe 1983; Loewenberg and Mans 1988). Gerhard Loewenberg and Thomas C. Mans argue that norms of courtesy and party loyalty flourish to varying degree in three European legislative systems: the Belgian, Italian, and Swiss parliaments (1988). They find that differences in party affiliation and personal ideology promote only incremental variance in norm attitudes and that this variance is consistent across time. A member's tenure and familiarity with the institution, however, greatly affects his or her norm perceptions—an indication that party and courtesy norms exist because senior members value and protect them. This research seeks to illustrate the connection between institutional familiarity and norm acceptance in the U.S. House, suggesting that Loewenberg and Mans' conclusions can be extended beyond the confines of a parliamentary system to the U.S. system as well.

SENIORITY

Barbara Hinckley's seminal work, *The Seniority System in Congress,* illustrates the disparity in member influence produced by the seniority rule (1971). She is quick to point out, however, that "the 'seniority rule' is a custom, not a formal rule" (1971, 5). The term "seniority rule" was coined as a symbolic representation of its unchallenged nature. In fact, the only rules governing the selection of House committee chairs concern the timely election of such and the recent restriction on the length of continuous service. Instead, the seniority rule is simply a norm, encouraging party leaders to select committee chairs by seniority in the given committee. For the most part, however, the seniority rule has been implemented *like* a rule. With only a handful of exceptions since 1911, party members have picked the member with the most years of continuous service in the given committee to occupy the chairman or ranking position. As Hinckley implies, this informal arrangement developed as a consequence of institutionalization, with the growing complexity of the House leading to member specialization and professionalization (1971).

From the 1910s through the late 1960s, the seniority rule was rarely violated. House Speakers had neither the will nor authority to override seniority and institutional sanctions existed for those who challenged it (Polsby, Gallaher, and Rundquist 1971). During this period, the House matured from a tentative, informal, less complex institution into a universalistic, automatic, impersonal one governed by clearly understood, tradition-based rules and norms (Polsby 1968; Polsby, Gallaher, and Rundquist 1971). Thus, the seniority rule, and other norm-related traditions, became both automatic and autonomous. It decentralized power, removing influence from the Speaker and party leadership, placing it in the hands of the most experienced legislators.

By 1971, however, many younger, less experienced members had become frustrated with the more senior members, specifically committee leaders. A number of important committees were governed by conservative Southern Democrats, who were easily re-elected, stayed in office longer, and occupied positions of inordinate influence as compared to more-liberal, junior counterparts (Hinckley 1976). By 1971, a majority of House Democrats, led by a large group of freshman, felt these chairmen were out of touch with the mainstream of the party. This dissatisfaction led to committee leadership reform in the 1971, 1973, and 1975 congresses. These reforms were a direct consequence of turnover, thus illustrating Weingast's claim that reforms arise to "further the interests of the legislators," in this case, junior legislators (1979, 246).

There were three reasons for junior member dissatisfaction with the seniority rule. First, committee and institutional structures "reward age and long service . . . which gives great power to those least likely to be attuned to contemporary needs" (1971, 3). Second, given the fact that seniority creates benefits, members and constituencies from safe districts are most benefited by this norm. When Hinckley originally made this argument, these were generally Southern Democrats and Midwest and Northeast Republicans. Finally, the seniority rule "obstructs party cohesion in Congress by creating independent power centers, a cadre of chairmen not responsible to party leaders since those leaders do not control their selection" (Ibid.). In short, the seniority norms allows senior members from safe districts, those "most likely to be out of step with current party programs," to deviate from the party with little chance at retribution (Ibid.).

Of course, these three reasons for junior members dissatisfaction also represent the advantages of the seniority system and the original reasons for its adoption. First, the seniority system rewards age by advantaging those members who establish the trust of their colleagues. Second, the seniority system benefits those members who get re-elected, thereby illustrating they understand the will of their constituents. Finally, the seniority system allows members independence from the party leadership.

As this dichotomy of opinions suggests, congressional norms can create a generation gap between members familiar with the institution and its norms and junior members who lack familiarity (Ibid.). Not surprisingly, interviews with members of varying seniority confirms that many junior members disagree with the seniority norm for the very reasons Hinckley suggests, while senior members cite several reasons for maintaining a system that protects the institution from both internal and external threats.

SPECIALIZATION

Compared to the seniority norm, students of Congress know comparatively little about specialization. In his groundbreaking research on Senate decision-making cues, Donald Matthews was the first to formally investigate the practice of member specialization, arguing that a Senate norm exists that encourages members to focus their attention and energy on "the relatively few matters that come before [their] committees or

that directly and immediately affect [their] state" (1960, 95). With James
Stimson some years later, Matthews expands on this argument to include
House members and the impetus for such behavior (1975). Matthews
and Stimson suggest that a member's committee assignment and time
served dictate the areas and extent of a member's specialization. Members with extensive experience in the institution are more specialized
and, thus, more apt to influence the decision-making process of other
members.

Interestingly, congressional scholars have also found that work in the
House mandates specialization to an extent not found in the Senate (Matthews 1960; Matthews and Stimson 1975; Hinckley 1988; Sinclair 1989).
Senators must be much more general in their legislative approach, due
largely to the increased number of committee assignments as well as to
the size and diversity of their constituencies (Hinckley 1988). Whereas
a House member is encouraged by the very nature of the institution to
become specialized, a Senator must wear a coat of many colors to best
represent his or her state.

Matthews and Stimson assert, however, that House members do not
merely choose to become specialized. In fact, "most congressmen are
forced to specialize—to focus their attention on one or a few areas of
public policy and develop some measure of expertise in these fields" as
a way of attaining influence, if only in a specific area (1975, 41). Hence,
a member can become influential by carving out their own area of expertise so that other members seek him or her out when making decisions.
For those choosing not to specialize, the opposite is true; Generalists,
those without the experience or desire to develop an expertise in an issue
area, have far less power to influence the decision making process of
their fellow members because he or she possess no specific knowledge
helpful to other members (1975).

It follows that junior members may believe that the practice of member
specialization is counter their interests because they are the least likely
to be advantaged by their committee or issue specialization. In reality,
by specializing those members can become more influential than by staying generalists. This research seeks to illustrate the dissatisfaction of
junior members by determining the effect that a member's duration of
service has on his or her attitudes toward specialization. Hence, junior
members may be frustrated by the House culture that forces them to
spend years becoming specialized in order to be influential. Conversely,
very senior members may be less likely than moderately senior members
to find specialization an important feature of committee work because
they are already influential and have no need to prove their expertise to
other members.

Interestingly, a new innovation of the 104th Congress demonstrates the freshman class's willingness to avoid issue specialization. Freshmen have formed several broadly defined policy groups, in which first-term members meet and discuss issues under consideration in an attempt to present a unified freshman position. These groups, The Blue Dot Coalition, Conservative Team, and Family Caucus, to name a few, do not rely on the specialized knowledge of more senior committee members. Instead, these organizations encourage members to take a stand on issues with which they have no practical or legislative expertise. The growth of policy groups is one of the three challenges norms face discussed in Chapter 4.

RECIPROCITY

Vote trading, the most obvious example of reciprocity, is a natural extension of issue specialization (Porter 1974; Matthews and Stimson 1975; Hinckley 1988). At its heart, reciprocity is simply accommodation. Members use issue expertise to form arrangements that allow one member to accommodate another member, thus furthering the causes of both (Hinckley 1988).

Again, Matthews and Stimson's *Yeas and Nays: Normal Decision-Making in the U.S. House of Representatives* provides the most fruitful analysis of reciprocity (1975). They hypothesize that issue complexity, time constraints, staff deficiencies, and a desire to be reasonable prompt members to adopt cue-taking as a way to make voting decisions. By cue-taking, Matthews and Stimson mean that members seek out information or opinions from other members with whom they routinely agree or hold in high esteem due to their knowledge and experience. These cues help the member to formulate decisions concerning how to vote on a given issue. They argue that cue-taking becomes a routine way for members to overcome the time and staff inadequacies which developed as a consequence of the professionalization of the House.

Using semi-structured interviews with 100 House members to accumulate the data for their study, Matthews and Stimson find that members often seek out colleagues with expertise and experience when faced with an issue with which they have little or no knowledge. This leads to a "cooperative arrangement" in which one member provides information and advice to the other and vice versa. Many of those interviewed mentioned this "reciprocal cue-taking" arrangement, suggesting that this is a widespread phenomenon (1975, 88). In fact, Hinckley finds that members acknowledge that "log-rolling" (slang for reciprocal voting for each other's bills) is so routine that it's "considered proper conduct" (1988, 110). Vote trading is also incredibly beneficial. Not only does it help to establish working relationships with one's colleagues, it also allows a member to secure his or her projects. This in turn can help that member win electoral support through distributive politics.

The committee system and the relationship between experience and both specialization and reciprocity leads to the subjugation of junior members however. Matthews and Stimson find the basis for this assertion by asking members from whom they take cues (1975). The data suggest that, above all others, members take cues from party leaders, committee leaders, and senior committee members. Not surprisingly, those least likely to be cue-takers are also those least likely to be cue-givers—junior members. In addition, junior members are the members least likely to condone the reciprocal arrangement that serves as the norm's basis. As Matthews and Stimson imply, junior members are the least likely to benefit from the norms of specialization and reciprocity due to their committee and legislative inexperience (1975). Thus, junior members are less enthusiastic about reciprocal arrangements because they are rarely benefited by them.

INSTITUTIONALISM

A fundamental building block of a norm-friendly institution is its durability—its ability to resist change. In researching the Congress of the 1950s and 1960s, Nelson Polsby found that the House of this period was highly institutionalized, possessing complex, durable, and bounded leadership and party structures (1968). These features worked together and independently to assure the continued dominance of a highly cohesive, institutionalized House promoting, but containing, political opposition.

The term institutionalism refers to the formal and informal organizational mechanisms of Congress. Polsby was the first to argue the establishment of an institutional hierarchy, promoting stable membership and professionalized leadership. He contends that over the life of the institution "[the House] has become perceptibly more bounded, more complex, and more universalistic and automatic in its internal decision making" (Polsby 1968, 92). As Congress became institutionalized, its values and norms also became institutionalized. Hence, norms like the seniority rule, specialization, and reciprocity became automatic and unquestioned. In short, members favored these values and norms because they furthered individual interests by extending member influence.

An institutionalized body "fine tunes its own internal structure in order to achieve greater effectiveness" however (McCubbins and Sullivan 1987, 84). Consequently, a movement away from a highly institutionalized Congress represents "a response to changing environmental conditions" (Ibid.). These environmental conditions can be both internal, as well as external. In Eric Uslaner's book *The Decline of Comity in Congress,* he argues that only the external factor should be considered, suggesting that the deteriorating attitudes and morals of member constituencies, forces outside the institution, are leading to a lack of comity within the institution (1993). Hence, members are more willing to challenge the norms of civility and comity, as well as other House norms. What Uslaner fails to address, however, is the effect that the member's internal self motivation has on these actions. Self motivation does not just include reelection, it also involves institutional influence and prestige, those things garnered through consistent and effective legislative work. This research will examine the effect that these internal goals have on the stability of the norms, despite the external posturing and rhetoric noted by Uslaner.

If it is true that members attempt to further their individual, party, and institutional goals whenever possible, then it follows that effective formal as well as informal rules are maintained until such time as they conflict with member goals (McCubbins and Sullivan 1987). The more effective institutional structures, those which allow members to pursue their goals with the least cost to themselves, are those that will endure, while new, more effective institutional structures will replace outdated, ineffective ones (Alchian 1950). This is not to say, however, that this is a systematic process. In fact, reforms often occur quickly, at the beginning of legislative sessions—sessions characterized by political turmoil, which create the desire for the reform. Thus, when members choose to reform the formal or informal rules, they are doing so because it is in their best interest to do so. And, they retain other formal and informal rules for the same reason. The member goals of today, longevity, influence, and status, are surprisingly similar to those held by House members 80 years ago, consequently, the mechanisms designed to foster those goals have not changed markedly (March and Olsen 1989; Stewart 1992; Loomis 1996).

This makes norms stable and enduring. Even in the early 1970s, a time of comparative instability, three senior Democrats lost their committee chairmanships, but another 21 went unchallenged. Why did so few senior Democrats retain their posts in a party dominated by junior members? A complete abandonment of the seniority rule would have been counter the interests of all members, junior or senior. A similar situation arose following the 1994 congressional elections. This time, two senior Republicans were passed over for three chairmanships, while another 16 went to the senior-most member. Again, personal and political advantages existed that saved a seniority-based system. In this way, its members gravitate to predictable institutional features, based in tradition, and forged by generations of their predecessors. The least likely to understand or appreciate these traditions are those members who lack a familiarity with the institution, or junior legislators.

Not surprisingly, the upheaval of the 1970s was in part an outgrowth of the ideological conflict between the liberal junior members and conservative senior members, often Southern Democrats in committee leadership positions (1976). The reforms were designed to usurp the establishment methods in order to replace these ineffective decision-making processes with less rigid, deliberative processes. This effort also represented an attempt to make Congress, and specifically standing committees, more responsive to public opinion and the membership (Stanga and Farnsworth 1978). In effect, however, these reforms empowered junior legislators at the expense of senior legislators.

The large entering classes of the 92nd, 93rd, and 94th Congresses brought young, aggressive, reform-minded liberals to Washington. "The newly elected members were impatient, eager to use their expertise, and unconcerned if they ruffled some senior members' feathers" (Loomis 1996). The revolt over out-of-touch chairs brought numerous changes including member autonomy, a redistribution of committee authority, increased staff resources, and the so-called Sunshine reforms that opened the policy-making process to public examination (Rieselbach 1994; Loomis 1996).

Ironically, the reverse was the case in 1995, when the House leadership was deemed too liberal by the newly-elected Republican Congress. In the first midterm election of a president, the opposition party tends to win House seats, around 10–15 on average. In 1994 however, this trend, coupled with a weakened President Bill Clinton and the loss of virtually every marginal district in the country led to the election of 73 new Republican members, many of whom were very conservative. Thus, the more-moderate (or even liberal, in the eyes of the freshmen) Republican leadership was replaced with much more conservative group. The subsequent changes affected not just the committee system but the subcommittee system as well, but again differed substantially from the Sunshine reforms.

In *Remaking Congress: Change and Stability in the 1990s,* Thurber and Davidson argue that another feature of the reform period was the rise of the subcommittee (1995). "The new rules reined in full committee

chairs," as the "subcommittee bill of rights" devolved committee authority to the subcommittees (1995, 17). The rule changes stipulated that
subcommittees possess a fixed jurisdiction and that relevant legislation
automatically be referred to the appropriate subcommittee. Thus, as subcommittee chairs assumed a more prominent role, subcommittees began
to usurp the policy-making influence of full committees. Prior to these
changes, subcommittee chairs had little flexibility to schedule hearings
or write legislation (Price 1978). Today, subcommittees "meet at the pleasure of their members, write their own rules, and manage their own
budgets and staffs" (Thurber and Davidson 1995). In short, as a consequence of the reforms, subcommittees wield greater influence by extract-
ing committees from the "arenas in which interests could be compromised,
brokered, and mediated" (Dodd and Oppenheimer 1993).

The reforms of the 104th Congress reverse this trend toward individual
and subcommittee influence however. Instead, the Contract with America
reforms empowered the party leadership at the expense of committee and
subcommittee chairs. These changes establish what they term a "condi-
tional party government," in which the committee system has become
secondary to the Speaker and other party leaders. Although they fail to
make this connection, Aldrich and Rohde essentially argue that the 104th
reforms create a Speaker-dominated system not dissimilar to the House
of the 1890–1910 in which the Speaker micro-managed the policy process through patronage and extreme sanctions for deviance. This connection will be discussed in more detail in Chapter 3.

Aldrich and Rohde suggest that the decision by a majority of the 104th
Congress to reform the committee leadership selection process was an
attempt to increase party cohesion, especially in the Republican Party
and secure more power for the party leadership, thus advantaging the
Republican members (1997). In a sense, Aldrich and Rohde are wit-
nessing the outcome both Hinckley (1971) and Jones (1970) predicted
some years previous, namely, that the committee system and conciliatory
opposition tactics constrained party unity. Hence, an effort to unify the
party dismantles the committee system and adopts a less-cooperative
inter-party relationship.

Reminiscent of the reform movement by junior Democrats in the 1970s,
the 73 Republican freshmen of the 104th Congress attempted to force
the party to remove restrictions that promote the interests of senior members over their own. On the surface, it might appear that they were
successful. On closer examination, however, it is apparent that the institution still utilizes norms and the members still rely on them. The institutional inertia demonstrates the continuing importance of these norms.

INSTITUTIONAL CHANGE AND NORM
STABILITY

As witnessed by the 1970s reforms, the institution does change. The reforms of the 1970s also illustrate, however, how much the institution remains the same. Despite high membership turnover, party switching, the perceived need for reform, and the ideological split in the Democratic Party, the three congressional norms under investigation, all of which subjugate junior members, were only relaxed and adapted, not eliminated. The same is true of the 1995 reforms. The Republican majority of the 104th Congress was dominated by junior members, including 73 freshmen, led by aggressive, young leaders, and perceived a great desire for reform, yet the norms remain. Why is this the case? The best way to answer this question is to discuss the challenges that currently face seniority, specialization, and reciprocity.

The first and most prominent challenge facing a congressional norm is the limit on committee chair tenure. Prior to the 104th Congress, the 103rd Republican Conference Committee, under the leadership of then-Minority Whip Newt Gingrich (R-GA), substantially altered the committee leadership selection process and laid the foundation for the institutional reforms of the 104th Congress (Gimpel 1996). The reform that best illustrates efforts to subvert the tried and true institutional methods is the committee chair term limit reform.

Originally offered by then Representative-Elect Jon Linder (R-GA), the Republican Conference rule limiting the tenure of Republican committee and subcommittee ranking members won approval by a 82–44 vote in the Republican Conference (*CQWR*, 12–12–92, 3783). This came only after a motion to create a task force to study the issue failed 65–76 (Ibid.). Fearing certain defeat, Democratic proponents, led by Representative Dave McCurdy (D-OK), chose not to introduce a similar plan in the Democratic Caucus.

The Republican Conference rule served as the blueprint for House reforms adopted on the first day of the 104th Congress. Several rule changes were proposed and voted on including an eight-year limit on the tenure of the House Speaker, a ban on proxy voting in committees, baseline budgeting, five subcommittees per full committee (with exceptions), and committee and subcommittee staffs cut by one-third. A full listing of these reforms and their effect on committee leadership power is found in Chapter 3, Table 6. The most notable of these was the committee chair term limit rule, applicable to all committee chairs regardless of party. The term limits proposal includes both the six-year limit on committee chairs and the eight-year limit on the Speaker. It was approved 355–74. All 228 Republicans voted in favor of the rule change while Democrats voted in favor 127–73. Not surprisingly, a large percentage of the members voting against the Boehner Rule were very senior Democrats—eleven of eighteen committee ranking members voted against the reform measure. The lone Independent voted against the rule's adoption as well (*CQWR*, 1–9–95, 122). Ironically, each of the senior Republicans who criticize the Boehner Rule in Chapters 4 and 5 voted for the reform despite their reservations.

Since the Democrats failed to follow suit in the Democratic Caucus, however, the rule does not apply to Democratic committee and subcommittee ranking members. Consequently, committee chair turnover serves to limit the experience-based power of Republicans and bolster the influence of the Democrat. For this reason, Representative Don Young (R-AK), former Chair of the House Committee on Resources, predicted his colleagues would reverse course, once it becomes apparent that the Democrats will not adopt the rule. "I'll guarantee it," he suggested (*CQWR*, 12–12–92, 3783).

The "Boehner Rule," as it came to be called, states that "no individual shall serve more than three consecutive terms as Chairman or Ranking Member of a standing, select, joint, or ad hoc Committee or Subcommittee beginning with the 104th Congress."[1] This rule weakens the seniority system as it relates to the succession of committee and subcommittee chairs by forcing members out of committee leadership positions after a given time period. The power to make committee chair selection was retained by the caucus, but, in practice, Speaker Gingrich exerted substantial control over all committee assignments (Aldrich and Rohde 1997).

In addition to the Boehner Rule, which allows the party to bypass the seniority rule after six years, freshman legislators have also devised a way to evade the norm of member specialization and cooperative reciprocity that arises from specialization. First-year members have formed the Freshmen Caucus, which meets to discuss the goals and interests of only the freshman members. In addition, freshmen have formed several policy groups based on their personal or constituency interests. These groups appear broadly defined and highly unified, encouraging members to adopt policy stances based outside their given area of specialization, thus usurping the specialized knowledge a member gains through committee work.

Deering and Smith compare these policy caucuses to those began by Newt Gingrich in the mid-1980s to capitalize on Democratic scandals (1997). In 1995, however, these freshmen groups are less concerned about the opposition than they are with furthering their collective policy goals. In fact, Evans and Oleszek argue that these groups served to complicate majority efforts to maintain party unity and discourage defections (1997). "Early in 1995, certain organized coalitions emerged within the Republican Conference, reflecting the differences among GOP lawmakers" (1997, 124). Groups of both moderate and conservative Republicans formed, forcing the party leadership to adapt legislation to maintain a majority (Ibid.). These groups not only frustrated Gingrich, Dick Armey, and Tom DeLay, but they also minimized the influence of senior, specialized Republicans. In short, the individual level interaction between members of varying experience and expertise was de-emphasized by the formation of freshman-only groups, which serves to weaken both the specialization norm and the reciprocity norm as well.

As discussed at length in Chapter 4, ironically, the challenges facing congressional norms illustrate the continuing importance of those norms. Not only does it appear that the Democratic Party will not adopt a "Boehner Rule" for its ranking members, evidence suggests that Republicans would disavow the restriction were they to become a minority party again. In addition, the member interview excerpts illustrate that junior members, even freshmen who disagree with the norms, *use* them when it is beneficial, most notably in the policy group setting. Thus, even in times of institutional change, the members still gravitate to the stability of norms.

JUNIOR MEMBERS

Given the previous discussion on the 1970s reforms, it is obvious that membership turnover greatly impacts institutional change. Why is this the case? As with other organizations, experience can produce influence. In the U.S. Congress, those with more experience rise to more powerful positions (Hinckley 1971; Polsby, Gallaher, and Rundquist 1971; Hinckley 1988). This has been the case for almost a century now, since the Cannon revolt in 1910. Recent reforms have caused some to question this assumption but through an examination of member attitudes toward congressional norms, however, it is apparent that those with less experience still feel subjugated by the institution's traditions.

In the pre-reform committee system, junior members had to bide their time on a committee until they were promoted to subcommittee chair and eventually to committee chair. This was part of the apprenticeship norm (Matthews 1960; Fenno 1971; Asher 1973; Smith 1989). Thus, the acquisition of power and influence was not immediate, it grew out of a member's institutional service. It is not difficult to understand why junior members encourage reform of methods that minimize their influence.

Institutional influence is an important aspect of a member's legislative existence (Huitt 1961; Manley 1969; Bardach 1972; Jones and Woll 1979; Dodd 1986), and to attain this influence, members must master the organizational politics of Congress (Dodd 1986). Influential positions—committee and subcommittee chairs, institutional leadership positions, party leadership positions—provide members with organizational resources attainable only through compliance with the institutional hierarchy. These resources include staff assistance, access to information, and parliamentary control; those things a member must acquire to significantly effect the policy process (Ibid.). Hence, junior members are less influential and less than enthusiastic about the legislative processes that they perceive as limiting their influence.

In his article "The Learning of Legislative Norms," Herbert Asher attempts to chronicle the socialization process of freshman members, and specifically that relating to the folkways of the institution (1973). He finds that "freshmen largely knew the general House norms prior to entering Congress" and little socialization was needed to initiate new members. Interestingly, Asher contends that the learning process appears unrelated to the member's previous legislative experience. Freshmen of divergent education, employment, and partisan backgrounds varied little in their understanding of the informal rules. In short, Asher finds that congressional norms are not unlike the norms of any organization; courtesy, deference, and loyalty are essential components understood by all members regardless of service time.

In Chapter 4, a re-examination of Asher's claim that the learning process is minimal suggests that the institution has changed substantially in this regard. The member interviews illustrate that both senior and junior members, including freshmen, cite the importance of the institutional education that takes place in the first three congressional terms. Given these findings, it is not surprising that junior members attempt to reform the institution upon entering it. Both the formal and informal rules restrict their influence and, since they do not immediately benefit from them or fail to understand their purpose, junior members advocate reform, if for no other reason than to level the playing field. In addition, there may be an idiosyncratic component to member attitudes toward institutional norms, which Asher also fails to address.

In studying three European parliaments, Loewenberg and Mans also came to the conclusion that an elected official's length of tenure was an important feature of that member's institutional understanding. They conclude that a members' "status," both defined by their party affiliation and their seniority greatly affected their interpretation of the institution's norms (1988, 197). While the research here does not focus on partisan differences in norm interpretation, Asher's research is updated regarding the understanding of the learning process. In addition to Loewenberg and Mans, Hinckley makes the same claim concerning junior members in the U.S. House (1988). She suggests "it seems fair to say that influence and deference still belong to those who have served the longest" (1988, 107).

As more senior legislators concede, members must undergo a socializing process that educates them to the advantages of traditional methods. New members may be resistant to these informal guidelines, but they are eventually "enlightened." Thus, those that continue to serve in the institution defend the norms that provide institutional benefits. The consequence of this enlightenment is an institutional inertia, in which stability is maintained even in times of change.

CONCLUDING OBSERVATIONS

The following chapters examine the challenges to and stability of three traditional House norms. As the previous sections indicate, norms are an important feature for both the member and the institution. They impart consistency and stability to the members and to a chamber once known for its instability (Bolling 1968; Price 1971; Galloway 1976; Peters 1990). More than simply updating an understanding of norms, this research illustrates the enduring nature of congressional norms. Despite membership turnover and movements for change, the norms that guide the institution adapt and survive. Why is it this the case? Comments by the members of the 104th Congress demonstrate that, as they are socialized into the institution, House members gravitate to these norms as a way of securing both personal and professional benefits.

This project relies heavily on the members themselves. They are the only ones who truly understand the positive and negative features of norm compliance. Consequently, it was important to interview a select group of members who would have special insight into these questions. In the next chapter, a complete description of the interview process and the issues surrounding member participation in the project is outlined. The research design, including sample selection, access difficulties, and the data collection goals, are discussed at length.

One feature of this analysis not found in similar research concerns the connection between norm compliance and institutionalism. In Chapter 3,

institutional structures that are designed to further the goals of the members by adapting the informal rules to match the prevailing attitudes are
broken down to show the connection between the norms and the institution. The decline of institutionalism demonstrates the connection between the membership and the norms, thus illustrating the effect that
membership turnover can have on reforms that change the norms.

In Chapter 4, this analysis is taken one step further to examine the
current challenges facing congressional norms. The three seniority violations beginning the 104th Congress suggest the norms have once again
come under the scrutiny of junior members. In addition, a six-year term
limit placed on all committee chairs effectively negates the seniority rule
for those members serving three terms as committee chair. Finally, the
growth of broadly defined policy groups suggests that the junior members who originated them are willing to sidestep the specialization and
reciprocity norms as well. Each of these challenges illustrates a feature
of membership turnover, junior member desire to alter the system to their
benefit. Interestingly, they also demonstrate the inertia of the institution,
an example of incremental change that ultimately does little to reform
the institution.

While party switching might appear to be a threat to the informal rules
of the House, it actually serves as an illustration of the power of the
specialization and seniority. Chapter 5 examines the recent phenomenon
of White southern Democrats switching to the Republican Party and the
effect these switches have had on the committee structure. Party-switching
presents several problems for both parties, especially the party gaining
the member. Most importantly, the party leadership must devise a way
to sidestep the committee seniority system so as to reward the party
defector while keeping less senior members happy. As a consequence of
seven 104th Congress additions, the Republican Party has developed a
series of party-switching norms that serve as the blueprint for future
defections—like that of Senator Jim Jeffords. These new norms are discussed in this chapter.

It becomes apparent why party switching and the changes discussed
in Chapter 4 ultimately have little effect upon the attitudes of the House
members in Chapter 6. When discussing the conceptual basis for each
norm, all but the most junior members cite the advantages and benefits
derived by their compliance. Hence, it is not an accident that the norms
continue to survive despite efforts to eliminate them. They continue because members want them to continue. The final chapter, Chapter 7,
summarizes the research and posits the future for congressional norms
in a more dynamic institution.

NOTE

1. The Boehner Rule is a subsection of Rule 14 of the Republican Conference Rules. It can be found on page 33 of the 1995 Republican Conference Rules of the House. The Boehner Rule, named after its most vocal advocate, Representative John Boehner of Ohio, was passed in December of 1992 as part of the post-election Republican reform package. At the time, it was not considered an important reform due to the minority status of the Republican Party. The 1994 congressional elections, however, changed markedly the effect of its adoption. The conference was given another opportunity to approve or overturn this section of the conference rule prior to the beginning of the 104th Congress. Given the large influx of new members, the Boehner Rule was once again approved. One point of great debate is the general interpretation of the rule. For instance, if the Republican Party loses a majority in the U.S. House, does the rule then apply to those former chairs who would be in line for ranking positions? Finally, similar debate exists among staffers with whom I spoke concerning whether a former Speaker of the House be allowed to continue past eight years in the event he/she served as minority party leader. The consensus suggests that the Boehner Rule would not apply to members if the Republicans lost a House majority.

Chapter 2

PROJECT AND METHODS

This study seeks to demonstrate the continuing importance of congressional norms and the reasons for such, as seen through the eyes of House members. In addition, it suggests an attitudinal difference exists between members based on length of tenure and posits a relationship between membership turnover and institutional change. Most importantly, however, this research illustrates the adaptability and resiliency of congressional norms. Each of these issues is explored through an analysis of interviews with 23 House members.

This is an important study for several reasons: first, the research found here challenges the modern application of Herbert Asher's claim that freshman members comprehend and appreciate the informal rules upon entering the institution (1973). Further, it substantiates the contention that junior members have different attitudes about the institution than their senior counterparts (Hinckley 1976, Loewenberg and Mans 1988, Gimpel 1996). This relationship between tenure and norm appreciation is substantiated and furthered through an analysis of the member interview excerpts in later chapters.

In his analysis of the 91st Congress, Asher argues that freshmen may *understand* the norms of member interaction, but by asking similar questions of members of the 104th Congress, it becomes evident that they do not necessary *agree* with the institutional norms. Thus, Asher's claim that members entering the institution both understand and appreciate the norms may be an idiosyncratic feature of his study or no longer appli-

cable. Instead, members without power and influence are those least likely
to favor the system that promotes qualities they do not possess—seniority
and expertise.

Second, this research formalizes the connection between institutionalization and the behavioral norms of seniority, specialization, and reciprocity. As the House became more professionalized it also became more
dependent upon norms of behavior because they fulfill the members'
desire for predictability. And, as the House became less institutionalized,
norms like seniority became easier to violate because member goals were
changing and a desire for predictability was being replaced with a desire
for influence and autonomy. Interviews with 23 members illustrate the
three congressional norms, seniority, specialization, and reciprocity may
be less inevitable in the 104th Congress, but they are still important to
both the members and the institution because they are predictable mechanisms of a stable institution. In effect, the norms have been altered and
adapted to fit the changing goals of the members, but the institution
retains them.

Finally, this research demonstrates the adaptability and stability of congressional norms through an examination of three current challenges to
the norms. In spite of membership turnover, reform efforts, and widespread criticism, seniority, specialization, and reciprocity are still important
to the members and the institution. Why is this the case? The members
themselves answer this question, arguing that norms help to further their
personal and professional goals, as well as further the institution's goals
of stability and independence.

INTERVIEW SAMPLE

This project and the analysis that follows owes much to the participant
observation and interview research of such past and current scholars like
Fenno (1978), Matthews (1960), Manley (1970), Asher (1973), Matthews
and Stimson (1975), Loomis (1988), and Whiteman (1995). In the following research design section, the discussion is patterned after Fenno
(1978), Matthews (1960), and Manley (1970), with regard to the issues
and topics to be discussed when utilizing an elite interview method.

The object of the member interviews was to establish an understanding
of member attitudes and gauge the general reaction to the norm questions.
In a sense, they were designed to see how comfortable the members were
discussing such an internal issue, while also noting their language and
demeanor regarding congressional norms. Consequently, the interviews

were designed to explore a difficult issue from the member's point of view and with his or her cooperation.

In Donald Matthews' research into Senate folkways, he employs what he terms an "exploratory" design in which a limited number of Senators are asked questions concerning institutional norms (1960, 269). Matthews argues that, given the subject area and difficulty in attaining time for interviews, "a limited number of informants was deemed more desirable . . . than a highly 'representative' group of respondents" (1960, 267). Consequently, Matthews only interviewed 25 Senators over a three-year period. In his research concerning House members and their constituencies, Richard Fenno observed 18 House members over a seven-year period. In an effort to maintain anonymity for his subjects, Fenno avoids defending the representativeness of his sample with anything more than broad generalities concerning their region and party identification. Hence, studies of these types rarely include representative samples or a large N (1978, 255). Instead, they explore a particular topic with a given number of elites in hopes to establishing some trends or patterns that may lead to further questions and analysis.

Although Richard Fenno's research is thematically different from Matthews, participant observation instead of directed questions, the same research principles apply to both. "Nothing better characterizes the open-ended, slowly emerging, participant observation research than this admission. . . . Whom should I observe" (1978, 253)? In Fenno's case, he hoped to observe members from varying parties, regions, district compositions, and political backgrounds. He readily admits that such a small sample cannot be representative of all House members or produce generalizable data. "I have tried to make it clear . . . that no claims are being made for the representativeness of the group—only for its adequacy in opening up the subject for scholarly inquiry" (Ibid., 254).

Similarly, Burdett Loomis also chose to forego representativeness in order to interview a specific group of House Members (1988). In Loomis's case, he hoped to interview the freshmen of the 93rd Congress, most of which were Democrats. Consequently, each of the 36 members Loomis interviewed were Democrats. As Fenno and Matthews did before him, Loomis defended this investigative strategy citing its exploratory nature (1988, XX).

This research design employs the same exploratory strategy witnessed in each of the previous examples. Like Fenno, a cross-section of House members is questioned, although there were difficulties selecting such a sample. For instance, given the mix of personalities in the House, how could a group be selected that was both workable in number without missing an important individual or universal characteristic? In addition, will the members who make up a representative sample be receptive to my inquiry? It was decided that quality and rapport should take precedent over quantity and representativeness. Consequently, offices of House members with which there was a connection were the first contacted. Again, this mirrors Matthews' design. In Matthews case, he began "by interviewing a handful of friends and contacts on various Capitol Hill staffs" (1960, 269). These contacts led to other interviews, until Matthews was able to interview 25 Senators. In this research, there existed contacts in a several House offices, including home districts, friends, former colleagues, etc. On the basis of these contacts, interviews were scheduled with six House members. Beyond the original six, however, requests were sent to staffers to schedule a short interview with their members. Since no specific connection existed to these offices, certain members were targeted that would add to the representativeness of the sample or provide a special insight into the subject under investigation.

The selection of these interview participants was based on several criteria. First, each member directly affected by the 104th Congress seniority rule violations were invited to participate. These included the three members who became chairmen despite a lack of committee seniority: Bob Livingston (R-LA) House Committee on Appropriations, Thomas Bliley (R-VA) House Committee on Commerce, and Henry Hyde (R-IL) House Committee on the Judiciary. Livingston's staffers scheduled an appointment on the spot. Bliley's staffers, however, were more difficult to convince. After protracted discussions with multiple staff members in Bliley's office, they agreed to a short interview of those topics previously discussed. Unfortunately, Hyde's chief of staff indicated that the Congressman's work on the Whitewater investigation limited the time he had available for scholarly and constituency appointments. Consequently, Representative Hyde was unavailable for an interview. In addition to Livingston and Bliley, the two members who were jumped for chairman despite being the most senior, John Myers (R-IN) House Committee on Appropriations and Carlos Moorhead (R-CA) House Committee on Commerce and House Committee on the Judiciary were invited to participate.[1] Staffers in both offices made the appointments without delay.

Second, appointments with several southerners were secured, including those Republican members who switched from the Democratic Party earlier in the session. This was important for two reasons. First, Barbara

Hinckley's seminal work *The Seniority System in Congress* explains the advantage southern Democrats had in capturing and maintaining committee chair positions (1971). Inquiring of southerners to see if they believe regional colleagues still possess this advantage was one goal. In addition, over the first 10 months of the 104th Congress, five House members and two Senators switched from the Democratic Party to the Republican Party. This presented some touchy but not unpleasant problems for the Republican leadership in both chambers. For instance, the switchers created committee imbalances and committee seniority conflicts on several House committees. Most notably, the switch of one 18-year House Democrat led to a rearrangement of committee and subcommittee leadership posts.

Hence, the inclusion of those most closely affected by these switches became a significant component of the research. So, each of the five southern Democrats who had switched to the Republican Party were invited to speak. Interviews were scheduled with four of the five former Democrats and one Democrat who decided not to switch: Billy Tauzin (R-LA), Nathan Deal (R-GA), Greg Laughlin (R-TX), Mike Parker (R-MS), and Mike Clement (D-TN). Unfortunately, Jimmy Hayes (R-LA) was unable to talk due to the time constraints associated with his run for the open Louisiana Senate seat. In fact, staffers for Hayes suggested that the Senate hopeful would only be in Washington, D.C., for a handful of days during the month in which these interviews were undertaken and those days were set aside for fundraising activities.

Third, an important target group included members with several years of House experience. These members would possess special insight into congressional norms and a point of view that differed from their less senior colleagues. Thus, twelve senior members were asked to participate. Of those, nine agreed to an interview. Again, the effort involved in setting up an interview with a senior member was more intensive than with less senior members. In addition to Livingston and Bliley, several committee chairs and ranking members participated including: Jan Meyers (R-KS) Chair of the House Committee on Small Business, Pat Roberts (R-KS) Chair of House Committee on Agriculture, Lee Hamilton (D-IN) Ranking Member of the House Committee on International Relations, David Obey (D-WI) Ranking Member of the House Committee on Appropriations, and David Bonior (D-MI) Minority Whip. Also interviewed were five subcommittee chairs: Myers, Moorhead, Tauzin, Michael Oxley (R-OH) House Committee on Commerce, and Dan Burton (R-IN) House Committee on Government Reform.

Up to this point, the emphasis had been on setting up interviews with senior members and committee leaders. Hence there was a need to include House members with less experience. Several staffers working for members of moderate seniority were consulted. Each of these three members were scheduled. Included in these was Bernard Sanders (I-VT), the only independent in the U.S. House. Representative Sanders was very important to the study because his status as the only third party member would give him an unusual perspective regarding the seniority system. In addition, interviews were scheduled with Scott Klug (R-WI) and Tim Roemer (D-IN).

Finally, the importance of freshman members in the 104th Congress cannot be overstated. Freshmen were the driving force behind much of the reform package passed at the beginning of the 104th House. In addition, they are the members most likely to support the challenges to the congressional norms discussed in Chapter 4. Thus, it was imperative that the freshmen perspective be included. Consequently, a dozen first-termers were approached. Ironically, staffers for freshmen were the most reluctant of all staffers to schedule time for scholarly research. Of the twelve attempts, only four first- and second-term members, including Sam Brownback (R-KS), Steve Buyer (R-IN), Tom Coburn (R-OK), and Todd Tiahrt (R-KS), decided to sit for an interview.

When all was said and done, 23 House members of varying parties, region, age, seniority, and committee assignments were interviewed. These included 17 Republicans, five Democrats, and the one independent. This distribution approximates Asher's distribution of 37 freshmen in his study of the 91st Congress (1973). Asher was constrained by the membership of the 1969 freshman class. Conversely, this study was constrained by the new Republican majority. The emphasis on committee chairs and those switching from the Democratic to the Republican Party required that the vast majority of interviewees be Republican. A full list of the interviewees and related demographic data can be found in Table 2.1.

Since this research only includes interviews with 23 House members, the first and most obvious criticism would be that the sample size does not allow for statistical analysis. Instead, this project utilizes a qualitative approach similar in method to Fenno's *Home Style* (1978). While undertaking the participant observation portion of his research Fenno also considered attempting a quantitative project. He ultimately opted for the qualitative design, saying "it was a deliberate decision to sacrifice analytical range for analytical depth" (1978, 255). The same can be said for this project.

Table 2.1
Demographic Breakdown of the House Members Interviewed

Member	Age	Length of Tenure (in years)	Party	State
Bliley, Thomas	64	16	R	VA
Bonior, David	51	20	D	MI
Brownback, Sam	40	2	R	KS
Burton, Dan	58	14	R	IN
Buyer, Steve	38	4	R	IN
Clement, Bob	53	10	D	TN
Coburn, Tom	48	2	R	OK
Deal, Nathan	54	4	R	GA
Hamilton, Lee	65	32	D	IN
Klug, Scott	43	6	R	WI
Laughlin, Greg	54	8	R	TX
Livingston, Bob	53	20	R	LA
Meyers, Jan	68	12	R	KS
Moorhead, Carlos	74	24	R	CA
Myers, John	69	30	R	IN
Obey, David	58	28	D	WI
Oxley, Michael	52	14	R	OH
Parker, Mike	47	8	R	MS
Roberts, Pat	60	16	R	KS
Roemer, Tim	40	6	D	IN
Sanders, Bernard	55	6	I	VT
Tauzin, Billy	53	18	R	LA
Tiahrt, Todd	45	2	R	KS

ACCESS

Given the connections in six offices, it was relatively easy to arrange interviews with these members. That being said, even those proved difficult to schedule. The reason for these difficulties, and most scheduling problems throughout the interview process, was time. As Lionel Collins, Chief of Staff for William Jefferson (D-LA), explained, the difficulty each member experiences is in how to manage one's time: "When my member isn't in the trenches, he's pressing the flesh." By "pressing the flesh," Collins refers to the continuous efforts to secure re-election. Hence, scholarly research must take a back seat to all other endeavors including legislative work, campaign efforts, and constituency service, the things that bring about re-election. This is especially important to junior members. Name recognition is vitally important to a member's re-election hopes. With exceptions, junior members are the least likely to have an established record recognized by their constituents. Thus, it is easy to understand why freshman members were the least accessible.

Due to the constraints presented by campaigning and travel back to the district, the choice of a time period in which to undertake the interviews was crucial. The month beginning in early May and ending the first of June was chosen. This was the legislative session following the spring recess. This part of the session is generally an important legislative period, characterized by numerous legislative markups (Oleszek 1996). Consequently, most members remain in Washington, D.C., until the summer recess. The interviews were undertaken during an election year, so this was one of the few continuous legislative work periods of the summer. It proved a good time for the interviews because only those members running for higher office or facing difficult opponents chose this time to campaign.

After selecting the days needed for the interviews, next came the process of scheduling, beginning with a letter of introduction to each prospective office. A generic copy of this letter is attached. In all but one case, this would prove to be the first of many contacts preceding the actual interview. Only one member, Patricia Schroeder (D-CO), declined immediately upon receipt of the letter. In all other cases, each office was called in an attempt establish a time and day for the interview a week after sending the original request. Often, more than one call was necessary. In fact, in several instances, three or more calls were made.

As suggested by the above list, the interviews were to be of a very specific set of members, so every effort was made to cultivate their participation. On several occasions, phone conversations and pre-interview office visits served to reassure senior staff members concerning the nature and duration of the interview. Unless specifically asked, the question content was not discussed prior to the actual interview. Again, Fenno's research in the 1970s provided the basis for this decision. "I presented as little as possible about the details of my project," Fenno explains, "only the few words necessary to justify a trip to the district" (1978, 259). He did so to prevent corrupting the member's responses by allowing him or her to anticipate the questions to be asked. In most cases, the questions and even the topic was left to the imagination of the staffer until the actual interview began. This was not always the case however. For instance, one chief of staff demanded a list of the questions for review prior to the interview. One was provided and the interview was granted.

Interestingly, certain days of the week provided the best opportunity for interviews. Many members routinely travel back to their districts most every weekend. Consequently, it is difficult to schedule interviews on Fridays and Mondays. For the members, most Fridays are spent in a plane returning home, and most Mondays are set-aside for return travel or catching up on constituency work from the weekend. Tuesdays, Wednesdays, and Thursdays were the three days that scheduling secretaries preferred when making interview arrangements. In fact, despite several attempts, no interviews were ever scheduled on a Monday or a Friday. Instead, the interviews were grouped, usually two hours apart, on Tuesdays, Wednesdays, and Thursdays. In fact, on the final day of interviews, a Thursday, six members participated over twelve hours. The last of which was that evening with second term Indiana Republican Stephen Buyer, who squeezed in the request during some early evening votes and a fundraising dinner scheduled for later that night.

The key was flexibility. The interview could happen when the member was free. This led to some interesting interview venues. While interviewing Bob Clement (D-TN), a series of votes were called. The first was a 15-minute vote (hence, each member has 15 minutes to make their way from the offices or committee hearings to the House floor to cast their vote) followed by several 5 minute votes. Clement was clearly enjoying the interview and wanted to continue, so he asked that it continue in the minority leader's cloak room just off the House floor after the first vote. After talking for another five minutes or so, Clement again excused himself for another vote. This happened two more times as other votes were announced.

Another interesting case involved Billy Tauzin (R-LA). After weeks of scheduling conflicts, Representative Tauzin was able to arrange a short interview late one afternoon. Prior to getting started however, the bell rang for another series of votes. On this occasion, Tauzin was already behind schedule and had other commitments following the votes, so he suggested that the interview happen on the way to the House floor. So, from his office on the first floor in the Rayburn Office Building, he walked through the tunnels underneath the capitol, all the while answering questions concerning congressional norms and his decision to switch parties earlier that session. So as to extend the interview, he chose not to use the electronic car that shuttles members from Longworth to the House. Along the way, he stopped several times to converse with other members and familiar faces.

QUESTIONS AND ANSWERS

The central challenge of this project is to formulate an investigative framework to research member attitudes toward congressional norms and examine the future prospects for norms based on these responses. Consequently, House member attitudes toward the three norms of seniority, specialization, and reciprocity serve as the basis for the research. The member interview responses should not answer these questions however. Instead, the interview data provides a window on the mentality of the member, an opportunity to view congressional norms from the eyes of someone personally and professionally affected by the implementation of these norms. This viewpoint should promote questions concerning the adaptability of institutional features and the reasons for their survival.

Manley's research into the workings of the House Committee on Ways and Means sheds light on this process. He argues that it is more important to have some "'mental pigeonholes' than a list of hypotheses to test" when you are undertaking an elite-level interview study (Manley 1970, 4). He quotes George Caspar Homans, a prominent industrial sociologist of the 1950s, who proposed that establishing a rapport with the subjects was the most fundamental component of such research (Homans 1962). "The strategy. . . . is intended to reveal something new in a relatively uncharted area, rather than . . . demonstrate what one is already pretty sure of" (Manley 1970, 4). The rapport thus becomes an important component of the interview process.

Richard Fenno, elaborating on and extending Manley's work, contends that member interviews and observation, "are less likely to be used to test an existing hypothesis than to formulate hypotheses for testing" (1990, 57). In that respect, the same can be said about the questions asked. No set question format is necessary, only a series of ideas addressing the topics under investigation are required. Consequently, there were eight subjects to be discussed at each interview. There was no particular order to this inquiry. Instead, interviews evolved according to the member responses.

The questions were open-ended and designed to encourage a free discussion of ideas. Table 2.2 lists the eight questions and the approximate order of most interviews. Often, however, the member was not asked a specific question because he or she answered it without being prompted. In fact, many members anticipated questions. In fact, one member, Tim Roemer (D-IN), spoke for such a duration and over so many topics that he answered most of the questions with his opening response. Others patiently answered each question posed to them, offering little else, except when prompted.

Dependent upon the circumstances of the interview—mood of the interviewee, the time allotted, and the conversation flow—each of the eight topics relating the questions listed in Table 2.2 were covered. Three

Table 2.2
Interview Questions

---

1. Generally speaking, what do think about the learning process of a new member of Congress? Is it easy or difficult to learn the formal and informal rules of the institution?

2. Generally speaking, do you agree with the seniority system with regard to committee chairmanship selection?

3. Please discuss your feelings concerning the new rule limiting committee chairs to six years of continuous service. What members do you think this rule will benefit?

4. What about the five Southern Democrats that changed to the Republican Party? Do you think those members should retain their committee seniority?

5. Have you found it helpful to specialize in a specific policy area? If so, is this specialization based on your committee work?

6. Another norm commonly debated by congressional watchers is reciprocity. What are your feelings concerning the trading of votes?

7. In your estimation, are the three norms mentioned (seniority, specialization, and reciprocity) as important today as they were when you entered the House (in years past)?

8. Finally, if the Democratic Party regains the majority, do you anticipate that they will eliminate the six-year limit on committee chair tenure?

---

members, Jan Meyers (R-KS), John Myers (R-IN), and Greg Laughlin (R-TX) allowed extended access that permitted several additional questions. On average, however, only the original eight were asked. Another member, Bernard Sanders (I-VT), answered the first two questions before becoming hostile and refusing to answer any additional questions. There was no provocation or specific question that brought about his reaction.

The eight questions comprised five general subject areas: seniority deference, specialization, reciprocity, seniority system violations, and party conversions. The members spoke freely concerning their impressions of these topics. They would jump from subject to subject, discussing anything that came to mind relating to the question. These monologues provided insight into the ways norms help or hinder a member's personal and professional goals. In fact, by asking the questions in this manner, the members illustrated how points related to one another and the effect a specific norm had on their legislative influence. For instance, Pat Roberts (R-KS) used most questions as an opportunity to discuss his time as a staffer for Keith Sebelius (R-KS), the man who preceded him representing the Kansas first district. From his comments, it was apparent that much of Roberts understanding of the institution came from his days as a legislative aid. Thus, he learned how to be a senior member and the reasons for certain norms while he was still a junior staffer.

The interviews lasted a minimum of five and a maximum of thirty-seven minutes, with a mean of twenty. All but two of the interviews were tape recorded so as to provide accurate quotes and allow for verification. The two interviews that were not recorded were of Minority Whip David Bonior (D-MI) and Ranking Member of the House Committee on International Relations Lee Hamilton (D-IN). Bonior specifically asked that the interview not be taped. Instead, notes were taken, which were elaborated on at a later date. Three different sets of notes exist, since on either side of Representative Bonior were two legislative aids writing down everything that was said. One aid appeared to be writing the questions asked while the other aid concentrated on writing down Bonior's reply. In Representative Hamilton's case, he would have allowed a taped interview, however, when the interview finally took place, it was on the phone. Consequently, notes were taken from the phone interview. A complete listing of the interview characteristics, including method, duration, date, and location appears in Table 2.3.

The use of the tape recorder was a point of personal preference. Fenno (1978), Matthews (1960), Manley (1970), Asher (1973), Matthew and Stimson (1975), and Loomis (1988) chose not to tape record their elite-level interviews. Instead, they took notes and elaborated on those notes at a later date. Fenno maintains he "is most comfortable interviewing politicians in a relaxing, conversational manner, without intrusion of mechanical devices that have be started, reloaded, and stopped" (1990, 81).

Loomis, admitting that tape recording the interviews was a viable option, chose to take notes and transcribe those notes. "I did not use a tape recorder, although most of the interviewees would have allowed me to do so. Rather, I took notes and wrote up an extensive transcript immediately after each interview" (Loomis 1988, XX). Loomis, like most researchers, did not address the reliability questions that might arise from the decision not to tape record the interviews when the option was available.

In this project, a conscious decision was made to risk the momentary delays associated with tape-recorded interviews in order to assure accurate interview transcripts. Not only did the tapes provide a record of the interview, they also served to create context for each question, help establish the interviewee's demeanor, and the general atmosphere of the interview. Finally, having a full and complete record of the interviews

Table 2.3
Interview Characteristics

Member	Date	Length	Method	Location
Bliley, Thomas	5-30-96	12	Tape Recorded	Member Office
Bonior, David	5-29-96	15[a]	Notes	Minority Whip's Office
Brownback, Sam	5-14-96	22	Tape Recorded	Member Office
Burton, Dan	5-23-96	17	Tape Recorded	Rayburn Room
Buyer, Steve	5-30-96	23	Tape Recorded	Member Office/Rayburn Room
Clement, Bob	5-30-96	19	Tape Recorded	Member Office/Cloak Room
Coburn, Tom	5-23-96	16	Tape Recorded	Member Office
Deal, Nathan	5-15-96	16	Tape Recorded	Member Office
Hamilton, Lee	5-14-96	10[a]	Notes	Via Phone
Klug, Scott	5-15-96	15	Tape Recorded	Member Office
Laughlin, Greg	5-28-96	37	Tape Recorded	Member Office
Livingston, Bob	5-30-96	22	Tape Recorded	Appropriations' Chair Office
Meyers, Jan	5-14-96	32	Tape Recorded	Member Office
Moorhead, Carlos	5-22-96	18	Tape Recorded	Member Office
Myers, John	5-15-96	25	Tape Recorded	Member Office
Obey, David	5-29-96	12	Tape Recorded	Member Office
Oxley, Michael	5-29-96	15	Tape Recorded	Member Office
Parker, Mike	5-23-96	11	Tape Recorded	Member Office
Roberts, Pat	5-21-96	24	Tape Recorded	Member Office
Roemer, Tim	5-23-96	17	Tape Recorded	Member Office
Sanders, Bernard	5-16-96	5	Tape Recorded	Member Office
Tauzin, Billy	5-30-96	10	Tape Recorded	Between Rayburn and House
Tiahrt, Todd	5-30-96	19	Tape Recorded	Member Office

[a] The length of this interview is estimated.

meant that the transcript could be re-examined some months later for additional insight into congressional norms that might have been lost during or immediately following the interview.

Other congressional scholars, including Rae (1994) and Whiteman (1995), have chosen to tape record their elite-level interviews to assure data validity. Of Whiteman's 318 interviews with staffers, only three were not recorded. Neither Rae (1994) nor Whiteman (1995) discusses their transcription techniques. In fact, neither even mentions the transcription process. In this project, the tapes were transcribed in the weeks following the interviews. Accuracy was imperative, so every word, including the questions, was transcribed in an effort to assure data validity.[2] Verbal pauses were not transcribed.

Interestingly, as the transcription discussion suggests, few congressional researchers utilizing elite-level interviews discuss reliability and validity concerns. Fenno (1978), Manley (1970), and Matthews (1960)

tions created the most consternation on the part of the members. With only these exceptions, however, the coding system helped to clarify member inconsistencies and provide a basis to determine those attitudes. When discussing the member attitudes in Chapters 4, 5, and 6, those members who gave indeterminate answers concerning the norm under discussion were not included. Instead, the discussion focuses on those members who clearly indicate their positions.

Fortunately, the investigative nature of the study does not necessitate a statistical relationship between tenure and member attitudes. Thus, indeterminate answers are not necessarily a hindrance to the research. Instead, they can be quite helpful. For instance, while it might appear that Representative Meyers was being evasive, her response could be viewed as an indication she is less comfortable discussing her opinions concerning the seniority system. Thus, the few indeterminate responses provided valuable data, for they suggest that the member views this as a politically sensitive issue, further validating the argument that the seniority system remains important to the institution and its members.

CONCLUDING OBSERVATIONS

As suggested in Chapter 1, the vast majority of the norm literature concerns violations arising from the House reforms of the 92nd, 93rd, and 94th Congresses. Unfortunately, this research rarely analyzes member attitudes beyond a superficial discussion of the factors that might have led to these violations. This research extends this understanding by asking questions directly of the members. The result is an expanded understanding of both the attitudinal differences between and among members and a link between these attitudes and the reforms that limit these norms.

In this chapter, the processes involved in collecting the data used in this project are broken down. Each step in the data collection required much time and thought. From the project's conception, the preliminary letters of inquiry, the efforts to acquire an appointment, the repeated cancellations, the actual interviews, and the transcribing, the project was based on the idea that a fuller understanding of the institution can be attained when questions are asked of those who work there. Thus, these goals are similar to the other congressional researchers utilizing elite-level interview, to shed light on an important facet of the institution that may be obscured through an analysis of standard quantitative measures.

In Chapter 3, the rise and decline of institutionalism in the House are examined, as well as the relationship between institutionalism and congressional norms. This will illustrate that institutional structures are designed to further the goals of the members by adapting the informal rules to match the prevailing attitudes. By tracing the rise and decline of both institutionalism and congressional norms in the 20th century, the connection between the two become apparent. The decline of institutionalism demonstrates the connection between the membership and the norms, thus illustrating the effect that membership turnover can have on reforms that change the norms. This historical examination will demonstrate the effect the stability of the institution has on the stability of the norms.

NOTES

1. John McDade (R-IL) was the most senior Republican member of the House Appropriations Committee, however, under Republican Caucus rules, McDade could not become chair because he was under federal indictment. Representative McDade would not do interviews concerning his attitudes concerning congressional norms and specifically the seniority system. He refused all interview requests because of the indictment.

2. A full and complete copy of the tapes and interview transcripts is available for inspection and verification. The author reserves all rights to any data collected, including the interview transcripts.

Chapter 3

NORMS IN THE HOUSE:
A HISTORICAL EXAMINATION

The U.S. House of today is much different than the House of the 1950s, as the House of the 1950s was much different than that of the 1910s. One reason for these differences is the elimination, evolution, and adaptation of institutional rules and norms. As March and Olsen propose, institutions have ever-evolving norms of conduct and decorum that establish a "standard operating procedure" for the time and situation (1989, 21). These informal rules, like seniority-based committee chairmanship decisions, serve an important function for they establish a sense of order and inevitability. First, with three violations in 1971, 1973, and 1975 and more recently with three in 1995, however, House procedures concerning committee chair selection have been altered, formalized, reformed and discarded, leaving the seniority rule less automatic than at any time since 1910. These changes are a direct consequence of a less-institutionalized House, where junior members are allowed to deviate from the standard operating procedure and discard traditional methods of congressional behavior in favor of untested institutional forms.

Among congressional researchers, there are two general viewpoints concerning institutional evolution. The first of these is the deterministic view, whereby membership and societal change force a customarily unbending institution to adapt and evolve. Not surprisingly, changes associated with idiosyncratic factors usually occur at the beginning of a new Congress characterized by high membership turnover. The deterministic view of House evolution centers on the four periods of quick, dramatic institutional change: the Cannon Revolt of 1910, the post-FDR partisan shift of 1947, the Sunshine reform period of the early and mid-1970s, and the Contract with America reforms of 1995. Each of these reform periods is defined by substantial institutional change over a short period of time, followed by a long period of minimal reform.[1]

In *Rediscovering Institutions: The Organizational Basis of Politics,* James March and Johann Olsen argue that "an adequate theory of politics must include not only a conception of elementary processes such as those organized by political competition or temporal sorting, but also systematic attention to political institutions" (March and Olsen 1989, 171). This theory of institutional change suggests that institutions are dynamic forces that provide stability and order for their members, as opposed to membership and societal order providing stability for the institution (Ibid., 53). This research integrates aspects of March and Olsen's theory while relying more heavily the idiosyncratic factors of membership and partisan changes that forged a less institutionalized chamber throughout the 20th century.

Given this symbiosis between institutionalism and effects of a changing membership, no one factor led to a less institutionalized House. In addition to gradual internal evolution of the institution itself, membership turnover has been the most dynamic element necessitating formal and informal rule change. Other factors, however, like societal forces, increased media scrutiny, and the collapse of the solid South have all influenced institutional change and reform. To varying degrees, each of the factors demonstrates what Uslaner termed "a decline in comity" and member cooperation in the institution, the fundamental components of a highly institutionalized House (1993).

Nelson Polsby and others argue that rules governing individual conduct and institutional procedures were most closely adhered to in the 1950s, when the House was most highly institutionalized, or bound by its rules and norms (1968). Polsby's research suggests that up until the late 1960s, the U.S. House was "perceptively more bounded, more complex, and more universalistic and automatic in its internal decision making" (1968, 93). Beginning in 1971, however, junior members and others subjugated by the internal decision-making apparatus sought to change or remove the inevitability of such decisions. As Rieselbach argues in *Congressional Reform: The Changing Modern Congress,* since these reforms and the reforms that would follow in 1973 and 1975, a perceptible decline in the institutionalism of the House has led to a far less predictable, less automatic institution (1994).

This chapter traces the 20th century evolution of institutionalism in the U.S. House and illustrates the relationship between the rise and decline of institutionalism determined by both internal and external forces and the rise and decline of institutional norms, most notably the seniority norm. As the U.S. House became more professionalized and its rules became more ingrained and infrequently challenged, the informal guidelines of seniority-based committee chairmanship selection followed suit. Conversely, as institutionalism lost favor with the reform Congresses of the 1970s, norm adherence suffered similarly.

INSTITUTIONALISM IN THE U.S. HOUSE

The basic premise of institutionalism is that governing institutions are important, and when institutions evolve, this evolution tends to further the individual and collective interests of the members. Armen Alchian was the first congressional scholar to make this claim, suggesting that a "natural selection" of sorts occurs within institutions that promotes certain institutional forms over other forms (1950). He further contends that this process is one of trial and error in which good forms are retained and bad forms are discarded. For instance, before 1910, House committee assignment decisions were the exclusive province of the Speaker; however, as members became professionalized and more dependent upon these decisions, procedures were altered to include a small group of party leaders and not just the Speaker. Contrary to March and Olsen's strict interpretation of institutional independence from external factors, Alchian argues that this change is an example of institutional evolution defined by member desires.

While congressional scholars argue that a relationship exists between the professionalization of Congress and the institutionalization of its rules, they debate which came first. Polsby, building on Alchian's theory, chronicles this evolution in *The Institutionalization of the House,* the foremost article researching procedural adaptation in the U.S. House (1968). Polsby argues that the two work together, stating that members became professionalized as a consequence of institutional change and many institutional changes have come as a consequence of professionalization. Specifically, Polsby suggests that certain leadership procedures that promoted stability also encouraged careerism, and members, desirous of career opportunities, adopted rules which furthered institutional stability. As a consequence of these changes, a career pattern developed that extended member careers beyond the two-term citizen legislator of the 19th century.

Polsby argues that the Congresses of the 1940s, 1950s, and 1960s were highly institutionalized, suggesting that the leadership and party struc-

tures were complex, universalistic, bounded, and linked to informal hierarchies (1968). By complex, Polsby means that "there is a division of
labor in which roles are specified, and there are widely shared expectations about the performance of roles" (145). By universalistic, Polsby
argues that "automatic rather than discretionary methods [are employed]
for conducting internal business" (Ibid.). Finally, by bounded, Polsby
suggests that "members are easily identifiable, it is relatively difficult to
become a member, and its leaders are recruited principally from within
the organization" (Ibid.). These three features work together and independently to assure the continued dominance of a highly cohesive, institutionalized House, which promotes but contains political opposition.

RISE OF INSTITUTIONALIZATION

Prior to 1880, the U.S. House was employed with farmers, business-
men, and lawyers, none of whom could be considered professional politicians. In the 30 years from 1880 to 1910, however, the House undertook
an amazing evolution from a citizen legislature to professionalized institution. This evolution is evident in Table 3.1.

In 1875, freshmen were 58 percent of the House membership. By
1909, however, less than 20 percent of the House were entering their
first term. The mean term of service throughout the period also suggests
a growth in careerism. The average House member served for less than
two full terms in 1875. By 1927, however, this average jumped to four
and one-half terms. Clearly, the institution had changed as the number
of junior members declined and careerist patterns developed. For congressional researchers, however, professionalization prompted the chicken
and egg question. Which came first, an institution favorable to careerism
or a membership desirous of institutional stability?

A number of explanations have been proposed to explain the rise of
careerism, most of which favor membership changes over institutional
factors. Specifically, Polsby's research asserts that several institutional
features made professionalization attractive to its members (1968). He
argues that, throughout the 19th century, weak House Speakers appeased
members by using their power under the Rules of the House to create
additional committees and make all committee assignments. For example, "to maintain his hold on the Speaker's chair, Henry Clay (1811–
1814, 1815–1820, 1823–1827) parceled out committee patronage so as
to satisfy the largest number of individuals and blocs in the congressional
community" (Silbey 1991, 203). Polsby argues that, over time, this increase in the number of prestigious committee posts prompted members

Table 3.1
The Decline in First Term Members, 1875–1931

Congress	Year	% First Term Members	Mean Terms of Service
44th	1875	58.0	1.92
45th	1877	46.6	2.11
46th	1879	42.3	2.21
47th	1881	31.8	2.56
48th	1883	51.5	2.22
49th	1885	38.0	2.41
50th	1887	35.6	2.54
51st	1889	38.1	2.61
52nd	1891	43.8	2.44
53rd	1893	38.1	2.65
54th	1895	48.6	2.25
55th	1897	37.9	2.59
56th	1899	30.1	2.79
57th	1901	24.4	3.11
58th	1903	31.3	3.10
59th	1905	21.0	3.48
60th	1907	22.5	3.61
61st	1909	19.9	3.84
62nd	1911	30.5	3.62
63rd	1913	34.4	3.14
64th	1915	27.2	3.44
65th	1917	16.0	3.83
66th	1919	22.7	3.74
67th	1921	23.6	3.69
68th	1923	27.1	3.57
69th	1925	16.3	3.93
70th	1927	13.3	4.26
71st	1929	17.7	4.49
72nd	1931	19.0	4.48

Source: Adapted from Nelson Polsby. 1968. "The Institutionalization of the House." *American Political Science Review* 62:144–168.

to seek re-election to maintain these influential positions (1968). Table 3.2 illustrates the growth of House committees during the 1800s.

For the most part, congressional scholars agree with Polsby's assessment of the internal factors; however, many conclude that additional, external forces were also influential in the growth of careerism. For instance, March and Olsen argue that the institutionalization analysis appropriately addresses the institutional factors as well as the external factors that led to careerist reform (1989). Aside from agreeing with

Table 3.2
Growth of House Standing Committees

Years	Number of New Committees	Total Number of Committees
1789-1800	4	4
1801-1810	6	10
1811-1820	11	21
1821-1830	6	27
1831-1840	6	33
1841-1850	1	34
1851-1860	1	35
1861-1870	7	42
1871-1880	4	46
1881-1890	3	49
1891-1900	9	58

Source: Adapted from George B. Galloway. 1976. *History of the House of Representatives.* New York: Thomas Y. Crowell Company.

Polsby's original argument concerning the rise and effectiveness of a self-maintaining institution however, congressional researchers tend to cite the idiosyncratic influence over the institutional factors.

Samuel Kernell, for instance, argues that "the decline in voluntary retirement, reflecting political ambition, was the primary contributor to increased membership stability" (1977, 49). He suggests that as the handful of political parties dwindled to two, the Democratic and Republican Parties began to dominate the electoral process, leading members to view Congress as a long-term career possibility. The consolidation of the party forces was apparent to congressional observers of the day, for as late as the 1880s, newspaper reporters "had to know what almost every member in the House thought about a bill in order to predict its passage" (Swenson 1968, 230). Only a decade later, these same reporters could consult with a handful of party leaders and predict the fate of legislation without fear of error.

Alford and Brady suggest that an additional external aspect of this evolution was the adoption of primaries and relatively uniform balloting procedures (1993). Prior to the 1870s, there was little oversight of election outcomes and polling techniques, prompting inconsistent results and corruption. Consequently, even those members seeking to challenge the voluntary turnover norm were not assured the incumbency benefits that define the present system. Thus, the adoption of standardized election procedures freed members to run for reelection.

Polsby, while not discounting the external impact, concludes that the opportunity to obtain prestigious, influential committee posts, coupled with several changes to the House rules greatly expanding the powers of the Speaker served to define the party, encourage reelection, collegiality and stability among the membership (1968). Up to that time, the only strong Speaker in the hundred-year history of the House had been Henry Clay, and, as previously suggested, Clay's power came from doling out favors (Silbey 1991). As opposed to the House of today, House Speakers were not seen as party leaders as much as they were institution guardians. This, however, would change during the 1890s.

Douglas Price extends Polsby's original explanation by suggesting an addition to the institutional argument (1971). Price argues that another internal component prompting the rise of careerism concerned the relaxation of the voluntary turnover norm. The voluntary turnover norm was an informal rule against running for a third consecutive term. This, coupled with the growing constituency stability, helped promote the internal changes suggested by Polsby. Price concedes, however, that the changing role of the Speaker also served to bring about this change suggesting that "the extreme fluidity or even chaos in the twenty-year span from 1875 to 1894 came to a sudden stop" with the adoption of the Reed Rules, a series of rule changes which consolidated the power of the Speaker and professionalized the House leadership (Ibid., 22).

THE "REED RULES"

No discussion of the institutionalization of the U.S. House can be complete without an examination of Speaker Thomas Reed's tenure. His actions as Speaker revolutionized the rules of the House, ushering in institutionalism and careerism that would dominate the next century.

Originally elected in 1876, Maine Representative Thomas Reed was long a scholar of Congress. His understanding of House history suggested to him that House Speakers since Clay lacked power over the minority parties, thus frustrating the will of the majority and stifling the legislative process (Smith and Deering 1990). Reed hypothesized that the continuing rise of the two-party system presented the Speaker with an excellent opportunity to assert dominance over the House.

Prior to the development of the two-party system, the House was an eclectic institution represented by persons of numerous political parties. Thus, the Speaker was elected through the efforts of party and regional coalitions working together to further their interests. Most Speakers found themselves beholden to multiple parties and regional concerns in an effort to secure policy and electoral support. In fact, Nathaniel Banks, Speaker during the mid 1850s, attempted to revise the rules of the House to increase the power of the Speaker, but "the committee of jurisdiction never reported the bill back" to the Committee of the Whole House (Bolling 1968, 53).

By the late-1860s, however, both the House and Senate were dominated by members of the Democratic and Republican Parties. As a consequence of the two-party dominance, House Speaker became a leadership post signifying a single-party majority in the House. No longer did the Speaker represent the interests of the whole House, instead the post-Civil War Speaker was the leader of a single political party which happened to possess a majority of House seats. Even after the 1860s, however, the minority party(s) in the House effectively controlled the legislative process through the use of the quorum rule. In the quorum rule, Reed saw an opportunity for the Speaker to assert political dominance over the minority and increase majority party loyalty (Swenson 1982).

The quorum rule was an unwritten rule, or norm, which allowed members to abstain during a floor vote without being counted toward the 50 percent of members necessary to legitimize the vote. If enough members abstained, a quorum was not present and the business of the House could not be carried out. The "disappearing quorum," as it came to be known, "was at best annoying; at worst, which was customary, it was a bone in the throat of an issue-oriented, serious-minded Speaker, determined to make the House work" (Bolling 1968, 55). Upon his election as Speaker, Reed, who described the disappearing quorum as "that system of metaphysics whereby a man could be present and absent at the same time," eliminated such parliamentary devices by instructing the House Clerk to record members abstaining as present (Ibid.).

Reed also consolidated the power of the Speaker by making new demands of party loyalty. He announced that James A. Tawney of Minnesota was to become the first Republican Whip "charged with keeping party members on the floor and voting in favor of the leadership's positions" (de Boinville 1982, 124). Capitalizing on the growing importance of House committees and the Speaker's power to select the members and chairman of all House committees, Reed moved to enforce strict party loyalty among within the Republican Party in the U.S. House in return for advantageous committee assignments.

In short, Reed revolutionized the House by strengthening markedly the Speaker and the majority party. In turn, party influence fostered member stability, which promoted professionalization. Careerism was the natural outgrowth of this evolution. As parties became dominant, constituencies stabilized, and incumbent reelection became commonplace; careerism developed into an attractive prospect. Not coincidentally, members began looking to the institution to secure the advantages of careerism, namely, influence, notoriety, and stability. With the rise of careerism, members "gave more personal significance to congressional organization, particularly the committee system" (Smith and Deering 1990, 33). They began to view committee assignments as a way to garner constituency benefits, thus furthering careerism, and, as the committee system grew in importance, committee assignments and leadership positions became too important to leave to chance. Thus, members sought institutional mechanisms which would assure committee assignment and leadership stability. As Figure 3.1 suggests, one way to increase stability, as well as influence and notoriety, was the adoption of the seniority rule.

By employing a committee system based on criteria outside the control of party leaders, placement within each committee becomes stable, almost predictable, based on the committee membership from the previous Congress. In addition, removing chair selection from the party leadership allows chairs to be more autonomous and less beholden to the party

Figure 3.1
The Relationship Between Careerism and the Seniority Rule

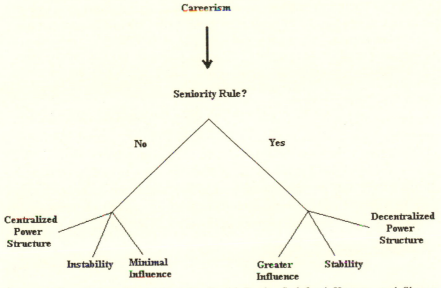

Source: Adapted from David Epstein, David Brady, Sadafumi Kawato, and Sharyn O'Halloran. 1997. "A Comparative Approach to Legislative Organization: Careerism and Seniority in the United States and Japan." *American Journal of Political Science* 41:968.

position, thus decentralizing the House power structure. Finally, the specialized behavior that extends from a member's consistent work in a given committee fosters institutional influence, so the seniority rule promotes a member's institutional influence. Thus, the seniority rule promotes membership stability, individual autonomy, and increased member influence. Not surprisingly, as members became more professionalized legislators, they sought the security and advantages of the seniority rule. Epstein et al. explain this relationship: "The rise of these committee-based legislative organizations [was] an institutional choice made by rational legislators deciding how best to regularize their career advancement subject to electoral and constitutional constraints" (1997, 966).

RISE OF THE SENIORITY NORM

As discussed in Chapter 1, the seniority norm refers to the institutional deference afforded members with more experience. This norm is the basis for the seniority rule, a informal ranking of members within each committee based on years of consecutive service to the committee (Hinckley 1971). The seniority rule dictates that the senior-most member in each committee occupy the party leadership position for that committee.

Prior to the 1910s, "seniority was only one of a number of criteria governing the selection of chairmen" (Ibid., 6). It is not coincidental that the seniority rule became the most important of these criteria as members adopted careerist goals. The seniority rule fulfills a number of member objectives arising from careerism, because it provides order and continuity, an adherence to tradition and decorum. The seniority rule "offers predictability concerning who has power in certain areas" (Ibid., 113). In addition, the seniority rule insulates the institution from outside influence by "creating multiple centers of policy influence" (Polsby 1971, 33).

Although the Reed Rules created the conditions for the seniority rule, it took Speaker Joe Cannon's reign (1903–1911) to bring about a revolt which would shift power to committee chairs. Cannon, a staunch conservative Republican from Illinois, fell out of favor with the progressive Republicans of President Theodore Roosevelt. Consequently, from 1903 through 1908, Cannon and other conservative members found themselves in the legislative minority, despite the Republican majority in the House. In addition, many senior Democrats and Roosevelt Republicans were gaining seniority and influence among their colleagues. When the 61st session of Congress began in March of 1909, Cannon set out to reassert his supremacy in the House.

Cannon began the session with a test of Republican loyalty. He delayed the assignment of virtually all committees for five months until after House consideration of the Payne-Aldrich tariff bill. He then rewarded members who proved their loyalty by placing them on the best committees. The returning members of those committees were simply bumped or reassigned as Table 3.3 illustrates.

Several fellow Republicans, led by George Norris (R-NE), who had been dropped from positions on three important committees to low-ranking positions on three insignificant committees, challenged the Speaker's power to make such arbitrary decisions without compensating the member. In March 1910, Norris introduced reform legislation that would strip the Speaker of committee assignment authority and expand the size of the Rules Committee. Progressive Republicans and Democrats both supported

Table 3.3
Seniority Violations in the 61st Congress

Member	Rank and Committee in 60th Congress	Rank and Committee in 61st Congress
Cooper (R-WI)	Chair, Insular Affairs	2nd, Elections 10th, Foreign Affairs
Fowler (R-NJ)	Chair, Banking and Currency 2nd, Reform of Civil Service	2nd, Reform of Civil Service 11th, Insular Affairs
Haugen (R-IA)	Chair, Expenditures Interior Dpt. 2nd, Agriculture 2nd, War Claims	3rd, War Claims 4th, Agriculture
Lovering (R-MA)	4th, Coinage, Weights, Measures 5th, Interstate Commerce	4th, Coinage, Weights, Measures 4th, Manufactures
Morse (R-WI)	10th, Indian Affairs 9th, War Claims	4th, War Claims 4th, Private Land Claims 6th, Manufacturers
Murdock (R-KS)	9th, Post Office and Post Roads	12th, Post Office and Post Roads
Norris (R-NE)	3rd, Elections 6th, Public Buildings 7th, Labor	7th, Coinage, Weights, Measures 2nd, Private Land Claims 6th, Revision of the Laws

Source: Adapted from Charles O. Jones. 1971. "Joseph G. Cannon and Howard W. Smith: An Essay on the Limits of Leadership in the House of Representatives." In Nelson W. Polsby, ed. *Congressional Behavior.* New York: Random House.

the reforms, which passed later that summer, thus revolutionizing the rules of the House by decentralizing institutional power.

As a consequence of the Cannon revolt, the formal power to make committee assignments came under the jurisdiction of party caucuses and select party committees. This change gave rise to the seniority rule. With a group of party members in charge of committee assignments and leader selection, the majority of chairmanships began to go to the most senior member of the committee. As demonstrated in Table 3.4, in the 60 years immediately following the Cannon revolt, only a handful of seniority rule violations occurred and most were compensated with lower-ranking positions on preferred committees.

As Table 3.4 indicates, from Cannon's reign to the late 1940s, the seniority rule was more of a guideline than a governing principle. As the committee system came to dominate the legislative process, however, specialization and professionalization of House members dictated the need for continuity. As a result, the 1950s saw "seniority emerge as the single automatic criterion for selecting chairmen" (Hinckley 1971, 6).

Epstein et al. argue that "committee-based seniority systems are established when careerism rises and parties cannot meet members' electoral and policy demands" (Epstein, et al. 1997, 971). As previously discussed and illustrated in Table 3.1, the number of House members making congressional service a career shot up from 1880 to 1910. Consequently, these demands increased substantially in a very short time period. Epstein et al. suggest that this quick rise, coupled with a split in the Republican majority, destabilized the customary process of selecting committee assignments. As a result, Progressive Republicans could not depend on the party to make decisions that would further their interests and promote career stability.

Despite the fact that the seniority rule was violated on occasion throughout the early 20th century, Epstein et al. claim that, in fact, seniority had become the organizing principle of the committee system. They contend that the vast majority of committees were organized by member seniority, but, occasionally, the chairs of less important committees were handpicked from the available, senior committee members, usually among the top three in seniority (1997).

Using a different measure of seniority, Epstein et al. show that, despite several seniority rule violations on less important committees throughout the early 20th century, the seniority rule became the automatic criteria for selecting chairs of important committees (1997).

As opposed to Polsby et al.'s measure of seniority shown in Table 3.4, which illustrates rule violations in chair selection, Epstein et al. dem-

Table 3.4
Seniority Rule Violations 1881–1969

Congress	Year	Party	Seniority Followed	Seniority Not Followed	Member Not Compensated*	Total Committees
47th	1881	R	2	37	25	39
48th	1883	D	8	30	14	38
49th	1885	D	21	19	12	40
50th	1887	D	20	21	9	41
51st	1889	R	20	27	8	47
52nd	1891	D	12	35	13	47
53rd	1893	D	25	24	9	49
54th	1895	R	13	39	9	52
55th	1897	R	36	16	5	52
56th	1899	R	42	15	2	57
57th	1901	R	49	8	3	57
58th	1903	R	43	11	4	54
59th	1905	R	51	8	3	59
60th	1907	R	45	13	3	58
61st	1909	R	42	18	10	60
62nd	1911	D	25	27	6	52
63rd	1913	D	33	20	7	53
64th	1915	D	50	6	0	56
65th	1917	D	45	10	3	55
66th	1919	R	35	22	3	57
67th	1921	R	44	15	0	59
68th	1923	R	40	17	1	57
69th	1925	R	37	22	2	59
70th	1927	R	43	1	0	44
71st	1929	R	38	7	0	45
72nd	1931	D	27	18	2	45
73rd	1933	D	38	7	0	45
74th	1935	D	32	13	0	45
75th	1937	D	42	4	0	46
76th	1939	D	37	9	0	46
77th	1941	D	39	7	1	46
78th	1943	D	34	11	1	45
79th	1945	D	37	9	0	46
80th	1947	R	9	4	0	13
81st	1949	D	19	0	0	19
82nd	1951	D	18	0	0	18
83rd	1953	R	17	1	0	18
84th	1955	D	19	0	0	19
85th	1957	D	19	0	0	19
86th	1959	D	19	0	0	19
87th	1961	D	20	0	0	20
88th	1963	D	20	0	0	20
89th	1965	D	20	0	0	20
90th	1967	D	19	1	0	20
91st	1969	D	20	0	0	20

*The term "compensated violations" refers to an instance when a member agrees to a violation in return for a low-ranking assignment on a better committee.
Source: Adapted from Nelson W. Polsby, Miriam Gallaher, and Barry Spencer Rundquist. 1971. "The Growth of the Seniority System in the U.S. House of Representatives." In Nelson W. Polsby, ed. *Congressional Behavior.* New York: Random House, 177.

onstrate that following the Cannon revolt of 1910 both Republican and
Democratic members of the House Committee on Appropriations and
House Committee on Ways and Means were seated according to seniority. This measure not only includes the chair, but all the members of the
committee. In fact, Epstein et al. find only one seniority violation for
these two committees from 1910 through 1930, and that concerned a
dispute between two low-ranking Democrats (Ibid.).

The 1947 Republican majority passed another series of reforms that
greatly reduced the number of House committees, thus making many
less-significant committees into subcommittees. Epstein et al. assert that
following the 1910 revolt, committee assignments to important committees were exclusively seniority-based. Consequently, when several less-
important committees were eliminated at the start of the 80th Congress,
seniority became the automatic determinant for committee seating on all
committees. Table 3.4 illustrates the dominance of the seniority rule from
1947 to 1969. In 12 different Congresses, there was one seniority violation
and that violation was compensated and did not concern a committee chair.
Obviously, the House of the 1950s and 1960s was highly ordered and very
predictable, suggesting that it was highly institutionalized.

DECLINE OF INSTITUTIONALISM

A highly institutionalized House is one with well-defined rules and
norms, understood and agreed upon by most or all of its members. By
1975, however, the growing number of junior House members, over
200 freshmen were elected from 1970–1974, were becoming disen-
chanted with these rules and norms for they promoted a policy agenda
out-of-step with the party mainstream. This disenchantment led to a number of House reforms designed to change the "automatic" nature of such
decisions.

Specifically, many of the reforms were an outgrowth of member dissatisfaction with conservative Southern Democrats' committee leadership. They were designed to upset the establishment's decision-making
methods in order to replace them with less rigid, deliberative processes.
Junior members argued that a system be developed whereby committee
chairs be selected based on competence, merit, and practical, as well as
legislative experience. The result was a series of reforms that removed
some of the autocratic committee control from the hands of conservative
committee chairs and disseminated that authority to subcommittee members and, specifically, subcommittee chairs.

Charles Bullock argues that these reforms were not only designed to

change the committee system, but also move the House away from institutionalism (1978). He justifies this argument by asserting that freshmen of the day had four reasons for these reforms. First, junior members
hoped this would "dispel public distrust" of the House, and restore public
confidence in Congress (1978, 209). Second, in a clear response to the
Watergate investigations, it was proposed that increased openness would
encourage members not to abuse their office. Third, junior members felt
legislators would work harder under the glare of public scrutiny, hence
the moniker "Sunshine" reforms. Finally, it was argued that increased
openness would dissuade members from following the traditionally powerful business and labor interests. So, in effect, these reforms were designed to "change the reference groups to whom members of Congress
respond" (216).

Bullock asserts that these reforms did exactly that. In a larger sense,
however, the reforms marked a general movement away from a highly
institutionalized House, characterized by close adherence to tradition. An
example of this change is the increase in floor amendments that followed
the reforms. Prior to the reforms of the 1970s, members rarely offered
amendments after a bill received committee endorsement. Hence, a procedural norm existed that discouraged members, especially junior legislators, from offering amendments. Since the mid-1970s, however, there
has been a marked increase in the number of amendments per legislative
measure illustrating the movement away from a highly ordered House.

Table 3.5 shows the number of floor amendments in the years before
and after the Sunshine reforms. A significant increase in the number of
floor amendments in the prestige and policy committees suggests the
increased intra-committee legislative activity, a clear change from previous Congresses where members rarely ventured outside their own areas
of specialization. Deering and Smith characterize these changes as a frag-
mentation of committee authority or a "decentralization of the power"
in the House, where committees are no longer the heart of congressional
decision making (1997, 183). The power formerly the exclusive province
of House committees had been disseminated to members outside the
committee in the form of amendment authority, suggesting a less highly
institutionalized House.

More recently, the reforms of the 104th Congress have further weakened the institutional nature of the House. To begin their first House
majority in over 40 years, Republicans introduced several reform measures that once again altered committee and subcommittee procedures.
Table 3.6 shows a full list of these reforms. Many of these reforms
weakened the power of committee chairs, but in a different way than the

Table 3.5
Number of Floor Amendments Per Piece of House Legislation

Committee	84th - 1955	88th - 1963	92nd - 1971	96th - 1979	99th - 1985	103rd - 1993
Prestige Committees						
Appropriations	2.6	2.4	3.6	9.5	4.4	7.7
Budget	--	--	--	16.5	0.5	4.3
Rules	0.0	0.0	0.0	0.0	0.1	0.1
Ways and Means	0.1	0.1	0.2	0.8	3.1	0.4
Policy Committees						
Banking and Finance	0.6	0.8	2.2	7.2	10.2	0.6
Education and Labor	2.1	6.6	4.1	3.0	2.1	5.3
Energy and Commerce	0.4	0.8	1.1	3.0	0.4	0.5
Foreign Affairs	0.3	2.9	0.9	10.1	3.4	1.4
Government Operations	0.8	0.9	0.7	2.7	0.3	0.7
Judiciary	0.2	1.5	0.8	3.4	0.4	0.4
Constituency Committees						
Agriculture	0.4	2.0	1.0	2.2	4.1	1.2
Armed Services	0.3	0.4	0.8	2.6	19.1	7.0
Merchant Marine and Fisheries	0.2	0.5	0.4	0.9	0.2	0.1
Natural Resources	0.1	0.0	0.4	1.0	0.2	1.0
Post Office and Civil Service	0.6	1.3	0.3	0.5	0.1	0.2
Public Works and Transportation	0.3	0.3	2.3	2.1	1.8	0.3
Science, Space, and Technology	--	1.2	0.7	3.1	0.9	4.5
Small Business	--	--	--	1.7	0.0	1.3
Veterans' Affairs	0.2	0.1	0.1	0.1	0.1	0.0

Source: Christopher J. Deering and Steven S. Smith. 1997. *Committees in Congress,* 3rd ed. Washington, D.C.: Congressional Quarterly Press, 205.

1970s reforms. Interestingly, the reforms of the 104th Congress helped *re-empower* the party leadership and Speaker, instead of further decentralizing influence; one of the designs of the 1970s reforms.

Rieselbach argues that the two main purposes of the 1970s reforms was to increase responsiveness and accountability by distributing policy-making influence to a larger group of members (1994). Subcommittee chairs assumed some of the duties of committee chairs, members took an active role in electing committee chairs, and increased committee staff meant more and better information for all members. These reforms represented an attempt to shift power away from committee chairs and back to the membership. Ironically, Speakers O'Neill and Wright both "exploited the tools bequeathed by reformers without alienating policy protagonists," but clearly this was not the desired outcome (Thurber and Davidson 1995, 5).

Table 3.6
Major House Reforms of the 104th Congress

Rule Adoptions and Reforms	Effects				
	1	2	3	4	5
Six-year term limits for committee and subcommittee chairs	X			X	
Joint referrals eliminated. Speaker sets "lead" committee	X			X	
Party leaders get enhanced committee chair selection authority	X			X	
Committee staff reduced by one-third	X			X	
House Oversight Committee establishes committee staff sizes	X			X	
Rolling quorums prohibited	X				
Proxy voting in committees prohibited	X				
Verbatim committee and subcommittee transcripts required	X				
Committee of the Whole motion to rise given to majority leader				X	
Members' committee votes to be published				X	
Most committees limited to five subcommittees				X	
Subcommittee staff hired by the full committee chair			X		
Eight-year term limit for Speaker		X			
Motion to recommit with instructions is to be guaranteed					X
Members' committee assignments limited to two and four					X
Three-fifths floor vote required to raise income tax rates					X

Source: Adapted from Christopher J. Deering and Steven S. Smith. 1997. *Committees in Congress,* 3rd ed. Washington, D.C.: Congressional Quarterly Press, 49.
1—Weakens the power of committee leaders
2—Weakens the power of the majority party leadership
3—Strengthens the power of committee leaders
4—Strengthens the power of the majority party leadership
5—General Reform

The 1995 reforms reverse this trend, for they are *designed* to empower the leadership. Most reforms, although again directed at committee chairs, shift policy-making influence to the party and, specifically to the Speaker and not to the membership, in an effort to enforce party unity and silence descent. Consequently, Speaker Gingrich in effect "appointed all of the chairs of House committees, ignoring seniority by sometimes passing over the most senior members" (Ibid.). Thus, numerous chairs felt they owed their chairmanships to Gingrich, as did subcommittee chairs (1995). In addition, Gingrich and the party leadership placed like-minded freshmen on influential committees and appointed them to important subcommittees. In fact, three freshmen, all Gingrich loyalists, were appointed subcommittee chairs, unprecedented in the modern Congress (Ibid.).

Thus, as opposed to the 1970s reforms, which shifted committee authority to subcommittees and the members themselves, the 1995 reforms shift influence from committees and subcommittees back to the party

leadership. For instance, the six-year limit on chair tenure will serve to
reduce the independence of committee and subcommittee chairs by making members beholden to the Speaker. The elimination of rolling quorums
(allowing chairs to call committee hearings with less than a majority present), proxy voting, and closed-door executive session committee hearings
without transcripts, will further strengthen the party by reducing the influence of committee chairs (Epstein et al. 1997).

While it may be too soon to predict the long-term effects of the committee and subcommittee chair term limits, the other reforms clearly cen-
tralize influence in the hands of the majority party and the Speaker.
Between "leadership control of the agenda, fewer staff, diminished procedural powers, more open committee procedures, reduced protection on
the floor, and the ultimate threat of simply being dismissed by party
leaders," the influence formerly left for committee chairs has been ceded
to the party (Deering and Smith 1997, 50). Recognizing this fact, Chair
of the House Committee on Judiciary Henry Hyde (R-IL) cracked "I'm
just the subchairman" (Ibid.).

In many ways, the reforms of 104th House are reminiscent of the Reed
reforms of the 1870s; not a further decentralization of policy influence
but a shift back to a more-centralized House. The reforms of the 92nd,
93rd, and 94th Congresses were designed to make committees and party
leaders responsive and accountable to the members and constituencies.
The removal of a predictable system for selecting committee chairs, the
strict enforcement of party unity and a reduction in an individual member's ability to influence policy, however, suggest the 104th reforms are
designed to make members more responsive and more accountable to
the party and, specifically, the Speaker.

The 1970s brought the Sunshine rules and the 1990s have spawned
the Contract With America. While neither stripped the House of all of
its traditions, both challenged the expectations and historic roles of its
membership. And, while the House is still a complex institution, it is also
a less bounded, predictable institution where discretionary methods have
replaced the tried and true automatic methods devised for smooth internal
decision making. The House of the 1990s is not the highly institutionalized House Polsby witnessed in 1968. Instead, it is an institution in
transition from the highly predictable committee-dominated system to a
far-less predictable individual and leader-dominated system.

DECLINE OF THE SENIORITY NORM

The movement away from institutionalism brought with it a movement
away from the seniority rule. The conditions that worked to promote

institutionalism as well as the seniority rule, minimal turnover, unobtrusive junior members, and adherence to tradition, became less predictable at times during the last three decades prompting a reevaluation of both. As Polsby suggests, institutionalism depends on relatively low and predictable turnover. The collapse of the solid South, however, coupled with two periods of high turnover led to a less-orderly and less-predictable House membership.

Since the late 1960s, the House has experienced the gradual shift from a solid Democratic South to a region of electoral flux. In *The Seniority System in Congress,* written before either reform era, Barbara Hinckley discusses the impact of the solid South on the committee system. She argues that more conservative Southern Democrats occupied an inordinate number of important committee posts because of electoral advantages, which subsequently changed (1971). The ideological gap between liberals and conservatives was exacerbated by the Southern conservative dominance of senior committee positions. In fact, Southerners composed less than 30 percent of all House Democrats, yet commanded 46 percent of House full-committee chairmanships (Mann and Ornstein 1982).

In addition, prior to its disintegration in the 1970s and 1980s, members from the solid South were elected and reelected without liberal Democratic or Republican opposition. Many of these members remained in office for decades, becoming the most senior members in their respective committees. Not surprisingly, Hinckley found that a gradual policy conflict arose between very senior, often conservative committee chairs and liberal junior members (Ibid.). After incremental reforms in both 1971 and 1973, by 1975 the mechanisms were in place to reverse this trend and replace the out-of-step committee chairs.

Junior members, a growing power in the institution, had little or no institutional or ideological interest in maintaining the seniority rule. So, in 1971, the growing dissatisfaction with conservative committee chairs led to Democratic Party reforms, allowing for a member to challenge a specific committee chairman if a total of 10 members requested such a vote. The subsequent vote, however, would not be confidential. The Republican minority followed suit, adopting a resolution stating that seniority need not be followed in minority committee rankings. In 1973, the Democratic Party committee challenge procedure was strengthened to assure a secret ballot, should a challenge be requested. In addition, three members were added to the Committee on Committees, the committee in charge of making chairmanship selections. Finally, in 1975, the power to make committee assignments "was transferred to the Steering and Policy Committee and all chairpersons plus chairpersons of the Appropriations Committee subcommittees were made subject to secret ballot votes in the caucus" (Ripley 1978, 126). This meant party leaders no longer had exclusive power to make chair appointments. As a consequence of these reforms, three committee chairmen were deposed: Wright Patman (D-TX), Banking, Currency, and Housing Committee; F. Edward Hebert (D-LA), Armed Service Committee; and W.R. Poage (D-TX), Agriculture Committee (de Boinville 1982). Table 3.7 compares the ideological differences of those Southern Democrats who lost their posts and those members who replaced them.

The three seniority violations of 1975, the first uncompensated violations in 32 years, validated the power and influence of the insurgent junior members and Northern liberals. In a follow-up article to her book, Hinckley argues that these violations were less about institutional change than about rectifying policy disagreements between liberal and conservative Democratic members (1977). In fact, she finds young members were attempting to depose old members and northern liberals were attempting to depose Southern conservatives. Regardless of their intent, however, the reforms that allowed for the seniority rule violations demonstrated the House was a less-orderly, predictable institution as a result. Ironically, both Hinckley, and later John Berg, argue that despite the disparity between the Party Support Scores, the members elected to replace

Table 3.7
Seniority Rule Violations in the 94th Congress

Committee and Chairmen	Seniority Rank	Years in Congress	Age	Party Unity Support Scores	
				1973	1974
Agriculture					
Old: W.R. Poage (D-TX)	1	38	75	41	24
New: Thomas Foley (D-WA)	2	10	45	81	80
Armed Services					
Old: F. Edward Herbert (D-LA)	1	34	73	22	15
New: Melvin Price (D-IL)	2	30	70	94	88
Banking and Currency					
Old: Wright Patman (D-TX)	1	46	81	50	51
New: Henry Ruess (D-WI)	4	20	62	88	84

Source: Adapted from John Berg. 1978. "The Effects of Seniority Reform on Three House Committees in the 94th Congress." In Leroy N. Rieselbach, ed. *Legislative Reform.* Lexington, MA: Lexington Books.

Patman, Herbert, and Poage did little to change the direction or ideological bent of the respective committees (1978).

As far back as 1961, N.A. Masters predicted the difficulties that might arise from high turnover and membership instability when he argued that the seniority rule is "ill-designed for flexibility and responsiveness to electoral changes and public opinion changes" (1961, 348). The changes that ended the solid South, the influx of junior members, and the Sunshine reforms that followed suggest a less-bounded institution, subject to instability. The relationship between the institutionalization of the House and the seniority norm is further illustrated by the decline of the seniority rule acceptance that accompanied the decline in institutionalism. Although Table 3.8 shows that only a handful of violations occur during this period, they are significant because they follow a period of strict norm adherence and are all uncompensated.

In "Seniority 1975: Old Theories Confront New Facts," Hinckley argues that the conservative ideology of three senior Democrats led to the three seniority violations. In part, however, this was also a statement about the members' age and ability. Each of the unseated members were

Table 3.8
Post Reform Seniority Rule Violations, 1975–2001

Congress	Year	Party	Seniority Followed	Seniority Not Followed	Member Not Compensated	Total Committees
92nd	1971	D	21	0	0	21
93rd	1973	D	21	0	0	21
94th	1975	D	19	3	3	22
95th	1977	D	22	0	0	22
96th	1979	D	22	0	0	22
97th	1981	D	24	0	0	24
98th	1983	D	24	0	0	24
99th	1985	D	24	0	0	24
100th	1987	D	24	0	0	24
101st	1989	D	24	0	0	24
102nd	1991	D	24	0	0	24
103rd	1993	D	21	1	1	22
104th	1995	R	16	3	3	19
105th	1997	R	19	0	0	19
106th	1999	R	19	0	0	19
107th	2001	R	19	0	0	19

Adapted from a table design of Nelson W. Polsby, Miriam Gallaher, and Barry Spencer Rundquist. 1971. "The Growth of the Seniority System in the U.S. House of Representatives." In Nelson W. Polsby, ed. *Congressional Behavior.* New York: Random House, 177.

over 70 years of age and potentially physically unable to fulfill their
duties. The relaxed seniority rule and the emphasis on member age and
ability also led to the 1992 seniority violation. In the middle of the 103rd
Congress, Kentucky Representative William Natcher, the chairman of the
House Appropriations Committee, fell ill and was no longer able to continue his duties as chairman. Mississippi Representative Jamie Whitten,
a conservative senior Democrat with over 30 years experience on the
committee, was the most senior Republican on the Appropriations Committee and thus next in line to be chair. The party leadership, however,
bypassed Whitten for Representative David Obey, a liberal 12-term representative from Wisconsin only fourth in committee seniority. The reason for this decision was age and ability, not an attempt to usurp the
institutional norm.

CONCLUDING OBSERVATIONS

This chapter illustrates the connection between institutionalization and
the House norms of seniority, specialization, and reciprocity, and the fact
that these norms flourish during periods of high institutionalization. That
is to say, that a complex, bounded, automatic institution provides a more
hospitable environment for norms than does an institution lacking any
or all of these traits. Hence, tracing the rise and decline of institutionalism in the House closely approximates the rise and decline of the norms
that rely on a complex, bounded, automatic institution to survive.

A clear relationship exists between the highly institutionalized Congresses and close adherence to House norms, as well as a relationship
between less-highly institutionalized Congresses and limited norm adherence. Through an analysis of seniority rule violations, it is apparent
that House norms are tied to membership turnover and leadership of the
institution, and as member careerism made the House a professional institution, the rules and norms governing the House were codified, leading
to strict norm adherence. Subsequent reforms, which either further decentralized institutional influence or centralized influence in the hands of
party leaders, disturbed the predictability of informal institutional
guidelines. Therefore, the stability of rules and membership in the institution affects greatly the predictability of House norms.

This chapter also outlines the growth and decline of institutionalization
and, with it, the growth and decline of institutional norms. The reforms
of the 104th Congress however, demonstrate that this is an ever-changing
process. In Chapter 4, the actual rule changes and institutional reforms
that accompanied the first Republican House majority in forty years are

examined through the eyes of House members. It is not surprising that these changes appear to further weaken the informal rules of seniority, specialization, and reciprocity. In addition, Chapter 4 challenges Herbert Asher's contention that members entering the chamber for the first time undergo only the most limited educational process. On the surface, these challenges may appear to indicate a comparatively unstable institution. In fact, the stability of institutional norms becomes apparent when viewed through the lens of party switching in Chapter 5. In addition, Chapter 6 outlines member attitudes toward the institution and its norms demonstrate its enduring stability, despite these and other challenges.

NOTE

1. At this early date, we cannot characterize the importance or extent of the 104th congressional reforms, nor can we predict how long this period will extend. Given the similarities between the 104th and the 80th House, however, it may turn out that this reform period will only last through the Republican majority.

Chapter 4

CHALLENGING THE NORMS: 104TH CONGRESS

Many questions with which congressional scholars wrestle can be addressed without ever speaking to a member of Congress, visiting a member's district, or even visiting Washington, D.C. Some subjects, however, demand information that only those more personally involved can provide; attitudes toward norms are such a subject. The research of Ralph Huitt, John Manley, and Richard Fenno found that the members themselves can make an invaluable contribution to a better understanding of elite attitudes and behavior, if for no other reason than it poses the questions researchers can and should be addressing in future research. Hence, the central feature of this research is the inclusion of member interviews. The next two chapters will examine both the challenges to and the stability of congressional norms, as seen through the eyes of those who must employ them.

Change and stability are terms closely linked to congressional reform, so much so that researchers often refer to one or both in manuscript titles (Hinckley 1978; Parker 1992; Rieselbach 1994; Thurber and Davidson 1996). This is a common practice for a reason. In general, Congress is a very stable institution with enduring characteristics. Yes, reform efforts occasionally succeed, but rarely do they truly change the institution. Instead, reforms are often adapted to fit the long-standing traditions of the chamber (Dodd 1986; Rieselbach 1994; Thurber and Davidson 1995). Consequently, while change can and does occur, institutional stability remains (Hinckley 1988).

In this chapter, the three such changes, or challenges, to congressional norms associated with the 104th Congress are analyzed from the perspective of House members. On the surface, it may appear that the reforms wrought by the Contract With America significantly alter the traditional, informal institutions of the House. But whereas altering the House rules may be relatively simple, changing the practices of its members presents a more formidable task. So while it is too early to fully assess the effect of the 104th congressional reforms, the characteristic desire for stability is apparent in the comments of most House members. For the most part, non-freshman members appear to gravitate back to the safety and predictability of institutional features they both understand and appreciate, despite reform efforts to abolish them.

Though generally supportive of the *idea* of institutional reform, many members challenge the method and extent of change brought about by the Republican majority. The comments of both Democratic and Republican members illustrate the contradiction that exists between the desire for institutional reform and need for simplicity and tradition. In fact, those strongly supportive of institutional reform find comfort in the institutional norms, whether they actually realize it or not. Even as junior members demand further reform, they speak of the respect they have for the knowledge and expertise of their senior colleagues. And, even as senior members endorse the reforms of the 104th Congress, they jest that their junior colleagues fail to understand the institution they are attempting to reform.

The belief that junior members fail to understand the House became a common refrain from more senior members. Members who have accumulated institutional experience argue that these changes may be good in theory, but in practice they defy over a century of careerist tradition. While it may be true that many Republican freshmen lack the careerist objectives of previous classes (Browning 1997), the majority of their House colleagues retain a careerist mentality, which institutional norms were developed to protect. These three challenges conflict with careerist motives by damaging three very popular and important institutional norms. In Chapter 5, a specific challenge, that of party switchers, is examined from the perspective of the members who switched as well as the Republicans adversely affected by the move. Chapter 6 takes this one step further by analyzing the reasons for the continued importance of the seniority rule, specialization, and reciprocity, in spite of efforts to eliminate them.

In addition to the three challenges to congressional norms addressed in this chapter, interview excerpts call in question Herbert Asher's conclusions concerning the learning process of congressional norms. Specifically, "The Learning of Legislative Norms"—Asher's 1973 article suggesting the existence of only the most limited congressional education—is reexamined. The findings suggest strongly that the complexities of the modern House mandate a more pronounced learning curve for the modern member than Asher found in the late 1960s.

CHALLENGE #1: SENIORITY VIOLATIONS OF THE 104TH CONGRESS

Chapter 3 illustrated the inherent connection between an institution's environment and the adherence to congressional norms. Thus, as the House has become less automatic, the norms that demand predictability have come under fire from those not benefited by their strict adherence. This change has occurred in increments, or spurts, over the three decades since the 1960s. The most recent of these occurred in the months preceding the 104th Congress.

Following the 1994 congressional elections, the new Republican majority, the first such majority in 40 years, continued the trend of sporadic seniority rule violations. Instead of strict seniority adherence, Republican leaders, and specifically Speaker Newt Gingrich, promoted three comparatively junior members to committee leadership positions. These violations suggest the continuing relaxation of the seniority rule and overall norm compliance.

The decline of institutionalism has allowed the House leadership to sidestep the seniority rule to an extent and for reasons not seen in the House since the 1910s (Gimpel 1996; Deering and Smtih 1997; Evans and Oleszek 1997). It is generally argued that the seniority rule violations of the 94th Congress, in which three Democratic committee chairs were bypassed for three less-senior committee members, was a result of ideological differences between the young, liberal, northern Democrats, and conservative Southern Democrats (Hinckley 1977; Berg 1978; Stanga and Farnsworth 1978; Hinckley 1988). In addition, Hinckley argues that the age of the three bypassed chairs contributed to the violations (1977). Interestingly, the three violations of the 104th Congress appear unrelated to ideology and more to do with institutional philosophy and personality conflicts.

John Myers (R-IN), the next in line for chair of the House Committee on Appropriations and Carlos Moorhead (R-CA), the most senior Republican member on two House committees, the House Committee on Judiciary and the House Committee on Commerce, were both bypassed for less-senior committee colleagues.[1] Given the historical parallels with the 94th violations, one might assume that these represent an ideological purge similar to those in 1975 (Ibid.). The evidence does not support this conclusion however. For instance, Moorhead possessed one of the highest party unity scores in the House, but he was bypassed for two members with lower party unity scores. Table 4.1 shows the party unity scores for the two members bypassed and those who became chairmen.

As the scores in Table 4.1 suggest, Moorhead was bypassed for reasons unrelated to his voting record. Myers, however, was more of a party maverick than Moorhead. That being said, Myers' party unity scores never dropped below 70 percent in the past decade, and rarely fell below 80 percent. Consequently, it is difficult for Republicans to make the same claim about Myers that Democrats made about committee leaders in 1975, namely that he is out of step with the party mainstream.

Myers argues that his voting record and age had little to do with the leadership's decision to promote Bob Livingston (R-LA) to head the Appropriations Committee. Instead, Myers argues that the party leadership simply jumped senior members with whom they had poor personal relationships or differing institutional philosophies. Specifically, Myers

Table 4.1
Seniority Rule Violations in the 104th Congress

Committees and Chairmen	Seniority Rank	Years in Congress	Age	Party Unity Support Scores	
				1993	1994
Appropriations					
Senior: John Myers (R-IN)	1*	30	68	77	75
New: Bob Livingston (R-LA)	4	20	52	90	84
Commerce					
Senior: Carlos Moorhead (R-CA)	1	24	73	98	97
New: Thomas Bliley (R-VA)	2	16	63	92	92
Judiciary					
Senior: Carlos Moorhead (R-CA)	1	24	73	98	97
New: Henry Hyde (R-IL)	2	22	71	85	87

*John McDade (R-PA) was the most senior Republican in the House Committee on Appropriations. McDade, however, is under federal indictment, and, Republican Conference rules state that he cannot chair a committee or subcommittee. The next most senior member was John Myers (R-IN).
Source: Congressional Quarterly Weekly Report, assorted dates.

suggests that the violation came as a result of a personality conflict between he and the Speaker that arose while Myers was the ranking member of the House Ethics Committee investigating ethic charges leveled
by Gingrich against former House Speaker Jim Wright. Myers also suggests his unwillingness to submit to Gingrich's wishes as Speaker-elect
damaged his chances of becoming Appropriations Chair.

> A year and a half ago, [he said] that he wanted to run every committee,
> meet with the chairman, . . . get his permission to do everything. I said,
> "Newt, I've served with five other Speakers and none of them ever ran
> committees this way, and I don't agree with you." . . . He even had letters
> we were supposed to sign that we would listen to him, which I refused to
> sign. I'm not signing any letter. He is the Speaker, but I represent the 7th
> District of Indiana, not the Speaker of Georgia. So, he and I are not
> friends.

It is clear from both the tone and content of Myers response that he
views Gingrich's decision as a personal slight unrelated to his political
philosophy or ideology. Moorhead, on the other hand, not only possesses
a consistently high party unity score but an excellent relationship with
the new Republican leader as well. Thus, Moorhead contends the decision to bypass him had less to do with ideology and more to do with
the fact that he was on friendly relations with many Democratic members
and willing to work toward compromise. The importance of both the
House Committee on Judiciary and the House Committee on Commerce
to the Contract With America reforms coupled with the party leadership's
desire to assume an aggressive, partisan philosophy necessitated the removal of the conservative, but non-confrontational, Moorhead.

> I guess as one of the more conservative members of Congress, I'm still
> quite independent. On some issues, I vote my conscience, but I do [vote
> with the party] a very large percent of the time. But I do retain judgmental
> decisions on specific issues . . . I have been one of the more supportive
> members of the Congress, but I get along with all the members, both sides
> of the aisle. [I have] lots of friends both ways. So, to me, it isn't adver-
> sarial. It's trying to work out the issues the best way they can be worked
> out for the country, and I don't see it as much as a battleground as . . .
> And so, to that extent there is a difference in philosophy. I don't think on
> issues, goals, there's that much difference.

Moorhead's concession that his cooperative nature and friendly relationships with Democratic members hurt his chances for the committee
chairmanships was supported by Tony Blankley, Gingrich's chief of staff.

"The Judiciary Committee has the likes of Chuck Schumer (D-NY) and Barney Frank (D-MA); the chair would have to fend off those people on a daily basis." Blankley argued. "[Newt] wasn't sure that Carlos was up to that" (Gimpel 1996, 35).

House members questioned about the violations generally believed that they were a result of either philosophical differences and/or circumstance. Mike Oxley (R-OH) contends that each of the three violations signaled the party leadership's attempt to consolidate its power over important House committees. "I think to a large extent Newt wanted to change the power balance to [empower] the Speaker and the leadership and this, in many ways, strengthened his hand where he had the ability to do that," Oxley explained. In short, the indictment of John McDade (R-PA), the most senior Republican on Appropriations, meant all bets were off in the Appropriations Committee, allowing the leadership to hand pick the person best suited for the post. Oxley was less comfortable discussing the reason for the Moorhead violations. After collecting his thoughts, Oxley shrugged and said Moorhead was simply incapable of filling either post.

> In our committee (Commerce) you have Carlos Moorhead who is a very nice guy but was not perceived as a real strong leader type, who also had judiciary responsibilities. He was on the Judiciary committee. And so I think it gave Bliley an opportunity, and that worked out very well for him.

While the information suggests that Moorhead's violations were based on his abilities, the reasons for the Myers violation appear more complicated. Myers himself argues that it was personal, but other evidence indicates that he was simply a victim of circumstance. Bob Livingston (R-LA), the member who ascended to the post, argues his promotion to chair had little to do with Myers. Instead, Livingston, who was still in law school when Myers was first assigned to Appropriations, contends that his leadership aspirations necessitated a compromise between the party leadership and himself.

> [That] was sheer politics. I was, in fact, the most aggressive [member] seeking a leadership position. One of the most of anybody who ultimately ended up with a position. It was in August of 1994 that I had a conversation with Dick Armey in the cloakroom, and he said, "You know, if we take the majority (never really thought we'd do it), I'm gonna run for majority leader rather than conference chairman." I thought to myself, and I shot right back, "If you do, I'm running for conference chairman." And with that, I gave myself an idea, and I ran out and talked to half the

members before the recess and the other half immediately upon coming back. I had spoken with every member of Congress before the elections on the Republican side, to see if I could, and I had about over half either leaning or committed to me. So I felt in pretty good shape for the election. Get into the election and what happened. And immediately after the election Duncan Hunter and John Boehner decided they wanted to run for conference chair. Actually I had a conversation with Hunter a few days before [the election] and, three days after the election, Boehner called me and he said, "Look, I'm running now, but I keep running into people who are going to vote for you. Is there anything else you want?" I said, "Well in my heart of hearts, if you ask me, I'd like to chairman of the Appropriations Committee. But I can't campaign for that because I'm not going to campaign against my friends." And he said, "Let me see what we can do." And he went around and generated support within the committee, with the members of our committee and among our leaders, prospective leaders. It was on the basis of his efforts that I got the job.

Livingston's comments suggest that neither Myers' differences with Gingrich nor his somewhat moderate personal ideology had much to do with the decision to promote the less-senior committee member. Instead, the decision opened a leadership position for a Gingrich loyalist, John Boehner (R-OH).

The evidence suggests that the seniority violations of the 104th Congress are less defined by ideology but are more a function of circumstantial and/or personal differences existing between the party and two senior members. Regardless of the specific reasons, these violations appear unrelated to an ideological chasm between the party and either Myers or Moorhead. Thus, they are different from the violations of the 94th Congress. Hinckley (1977), Berg (1978), Stanga and Farnsworth (1978), among others argue that the 94th Congress violations were the result of an ideological rift in the Democratic Party between the senior Democrats chairing several House committees and their more liberal northern colleagues. In this case, Gingrich seemingly created a power that did not exist prior to his election as Speaker. As Chris Cox (R-CA) described it, "here in the House, this is a one man show. . . . Gingrich has given [committee chairs] a renewed sense that chairs serve at the Speaker's pleasure" (Gimpel 1996, 36).

The Speaker's power to make such arbitrary selections has not existed since the era of the powerful speaker (1890–1910), ending with the Cannon Revolt (Pitney and Connelly 1995). Clearly, this presents a new and dangerous challenge to the seniority system. When put in context, however, the Gingrich violations also illustrate the continuing importance, or stability, of seniority-based committee leadership selection. First, despite the fact that the vast majority of Gingrich's House supporters were junior Republicans, and over 50 percent of House Republicans have less than three terms of House experience, he still only bypassed two senior Republicans. In that sense, it is the violations that did *not* occur that shed light on the stability of the institution's norms.

Of 19 congressional committees, Speaker Gingrich and the Republican leadership endorsed the most senior Republican member 16 times, included on this list is Gerald Solomon (R-NY). Solomon, a nine-term Republican and senior Republican on the Rules Committee, was the only Republican to challenge Gingrich for the party leadership post in the fall of 1994. Although Solomon later removed his name from consideration, the effort to unseat Gingrich could not have endeared Solomon to the future Speaker. Despite this fact, Gingrich chose to support Solomon's candidacy for the Rules Committee chairmanship (*CQWR*, 11–19–94, 3326).

In addition, Gingrich and the party leadership endorsed the chairmanship of three moderate, senior Republicans, Benjamin Gilman (R-NY), Jan Meyers (R-KS), and William Clinger (R-PA). Gilman, especially, illustrates the leadership's reluctance to further challenge the seniority rule. As the most senior Republican on the House Committee on International Relations, Gilman, a 12-term member from New York, is one of the few Rockefeller Republicans remaining from the early 1970s. In 1993, in fact, Gilman had a party unity score of 53 percent, the second lowest among all House Republicans. Despite Gilman's moderate ideology, Gingrich and the Republican leadership decided three seniority violations were enough and endorsed his run for the chairmanship of an important House policy committee.

While interviews with Myers and Livingston indicate that the 104th violations were less about ideology and more about personality and politics, the stability of the institution is once again validated with the 16 selections that fail to challenge the seniority rule. Even with a party leadership and Speaker powerful enough to remove a potential chair because of a personality conflict or for political gain, they are still compelled to abide by the institution's seniority norm. The fact that a handful of liberal Republicans were chosen to chair important committees is the best illustration that the seniority rule is still important to the members.

CHALLENGE #2: THE "BOEHNER RULE"

In addition to three seniority violations pushed by the party leadership, every House Republican voted to institute a reform package that greatly increases the power of the majority party leadership at the expense of committee leaders. The most important of these changes may be the limit on committee chair tenure, passed the first day of the 104th Congress. Known as the Boehner Rule, it establishes limits on seniority-based committee chairmanships, thus weakening one of the most sacred committee traditions.

The reforms of the 1970s, especially those associated with the Class of 1974, originally undermined the long-subscribed-to norms of congressional behavior. The 92nd, 93rd, and 94th freshman classes challenged the omnipotent power of committee chairmen through a series of reforms aimed at forcing chairs to be more responsive to the membership, including conference and caucus elections of committee leaders. Numerous congressional scholars attribute these reforms to the polarization that occurred between the careerist members (those members with 10 or more terms in office) and junior members (those with 3 or fewer terms), who found they had little power to influence the policy process and the ideological differences existing between the two groups (Hinckley 1977; Berg 1978; Stanga and Farnsworth 1978; Rieselbach 1978; Hinckley 1988; Loomis 1996).

Many of the conditions that brought about the 1970s reforms once again surfaced as the 1990s approached. Rieselbach suggests an idiosyncratic explanation for these for the latter reforms (1995). Instead of the internal forces fostering reform, namely changing membership, Rieselbach argues that public dissatisfaction over the Post Office scandal and other indiscretions led members to adopt reformist leanings (1995). For the most part, however, these efforts were unsuccessful until the Contract with America. Although it may be true that constituency pressures were driving some reformists, it seems likely that the institutional change that occurred in 1995 was less circumstantial and more a result of changing membership. As Evans and Oleszek point out, these reforms were not adopted in 1991, the first election after the House bank scandal and Wright speakership. Instead, they were adopted some years later, when a sufficient number of new members had entered the institution (1997).

Thus, the large Republican turnover beginning with the 1992 House election, coupled with the steady increase in careerist members throughout the 1980s, helped to foster several reforms reminiscent of the 1970s reforms. As in the late 1960s, the House of the 1980s and early 1990s became dominated by senior members. In fact, the average length of tenure for members in the 102nd Congress had risen to 6.2 terms, up from 4.6 terms in the 95th Congress. Table 4.2 illustrates this trend. The vast increase in the number of junior members beginning in 1992 and increasing substantially in 1994 brought this mean back to 4.8 terms in the span of only two terms.

Table 4.2
Seniority of House Members, 1969–1995

Congress	Freshman	Freshman %	1-3 Terms	1-3 Terms %	10+ Terms	10+ Terms %	Mean Term
91st - 1969	36	8	159	37	76	18	5.7
92d - 1971	48	11	150	34	87	20	6.0
93rd - 1973	67	16	157	37	78	18	5.7
94th - 1975	86	20	189	44	61	14	5.4
95th - 1977	64	15	210	48	60	14	4.6
96th - 1979	77	18	214	49	55	13	5.0
97th - 1981	73	17	205	47	50	11	4.9
98th - 1983	80	18	211	49	55	13	4.6
99th - 1985	39	9	180	41	59	14	4.7
100th - 1987	48	11	159	37	69	16	5.6
101st - 1989	33	8	120	28	60	14	5.8
102d - 1991	42	10	130	30	76	17	6.2
103rd - 1993	110	25	187	43	67	15	5.3
104th - 1995	86	20	225	52	59	14	4.8

Source: Ornstein, Norman J., Thomas E. Mann, and Michael J. Malbin. *Vital Statistics on Congress 1995–1996.* Washington, D.C.: Congressional Quarterly Inc.

On closer analysis, Table 4.2 illustrates the trends that have dominated the congressional reform process in the House since the 1960s. The sharp increase in junior members, a consequence of the large freshman classes in 1973 and 1975, led to the three seniority rule violations prior to the 94th Congress and the reforms that accompanied these violations. Interestingly, at the time, some congressional scholars argued that the retirements and incumbent losses in the 1970s were symptomatic of an institutional shift away from the careerist politician. "The decline of seniority in Congress may permit talent to be substituted by age," argued Aaron Wildavsky. "It also guarantees that Congress will provide less attractive careers" (1975, 62–63). Similarly, John Hibbing concluded that in the future "careerism will not be prevalent, and, in fact, will probably be as rare as it was in the 1930s and 1940s" (1982, 72). Clearly, these assessments were incorrect. Throughout the 1980s, few members opted for voluntary retirement, thus creating small entering classes and limited turnover.

The small classes throughout the mid to late 1980s laid the groundwork for another period of reform. By 1990, over 70 percent of the House had more than three terms of experience. Once again, two large freshman classes, the 103rd and 104th Congresses, led to the reform atmosphere and another challenge to the seniority rule. The historical trends leading to congressional reform are discussed more extensively in Sundquist (1981), Sheppard (1985), and Sinclair (1989; 1995). In this vein, the Boehner Rule is simply the latest incarnation of seniority system reform.

Originally offered by then-freshman Representative-Elect Jon Linder (R-GA), the Republican Conference rule limiting the tenure of Republican committee and subcommittee ranking members won approval by a 82–44 vote in the Republican Conference, after a motion to create a task force to study the issue failed 65–76 (*CQWR*, 12–12–92, 3783). Fearing certain defeat in the Democratic Caucus, Democratic proponents, led by Representative Dave McCurdy (D-OK), chose not to introduce a similar plan in the Democratic Caucus. Unlike the Republican Party, which witnessed substantial turnover in both 1992 and 1994, the Democratic Party grew markedly in 1992 and stabilized again in 1994. Thus, the Democratic Party did not implement reforms similar to those pushed by junior Republicans.

The Republican Conference rule served as the blueprint for the reforms adopted by the entire full House on the first day of the 104th Congress. In addition to the committee chair term limit, other rule changes included an eight year limit on the tenure of the House Speaker, a ban on proxy voting in committees, baseline budgeting, five subcommittees per full committee (with exceptions), and committee and subcommittee staffs cut by one-third. For a complete list of the 104th reforms, see Chapter 3, Table 3–6. The committee chair term limit proposal became a House rule, applicable to all committee chairs regardless of party, when it won final approval 355–74. All 228 Republicans voted in favor of the rule change, while Democrats voted in favor 127–73. Not surprisingly, a large percentage of those who voted against the Boehner Rule were very senior Democrats; in fact, 11 of 18 committee ranking members voted against the reform. The lone Independent voted against the rule's adoption (*CQWR*, 1–7–95, 122).

The Democrats failed to follow suit in the Democratic Caucus, however, so the limit does not apply to Democratic committee and subcommittee ranking members. Hence, committee chair turnover potentially serves to limit the experience-based influence of Republican leaders and bolster the similar power of the Democratic leaders. For that reason, Representative Don Young (R-AK), Chairman of the House Committee on Resources, predicted that his colleagues would reverse course within the next six years, once it becomes apparent that the Democrats will not adopt the rule. "I'll guarantee it," he suggested (*CQWR*, 12–12–92, 3783).

The "Boehner Rule," as it came to be called, states that "no individual shall serve more than three consecutive terms as Chairman or Ranking Member of a standing, select, joint, or ad hoc Committee or Subcommittee beginning with the 104th Congress" (Rule 14 Subsection, p. 33, 1995 House Republican Conference Rules). The rule, named after its author and most vocal advocate, Representative John Boehner (R-OH), was passed in December of 1992 as part of the post-election Republican reform package. At the time, it was not considered an important reform due to the minority status of the Republican Party. With the 1994 congressional elections, however, the import of its adoption increased markedly. The conference was given another opportunity to approve or overturn this section of the conference rule prior to the beginning of the 104th Congress, and, given the large influx of new members, the Boehner Rule was once again approved without sizeable opposition.

One point of great debate, however, is the general interpretation of the Boehner Rule and the accompanying rule limiting the Speaker to only eight years of continuous service. For instance, if the Republican Party loses a majority in the U.S. House, does the rule then apply to those former chairs in line for ranking positions? Similarly, would a former Speaker of the House, such as Newt Gingrich, be allowed to continue past eight years in the event he/she served as minority party leader? The consensus of those interviewed suggests that the Boehner Rule would not apply to members if the Republicans lost the House majority. The desire to revert back to the long-standing institutional norms in times of uncertainty once again emphasizes the stability of these norms. Many members and staffers suggested that this might happen regardless. For instance, when asked whether the Republicans would abandon the committee and subcommittee chair term limits if they retain the majority for six years, Minority Whip David Bonior (D-MI) quipped, "What do *you* think?"

Until the reform is reformed, however, the Boehner rule potentially negates the seniority system as it relates to the succession of committee and subcommittee chairs by forcing members out of committee leadership positions after a given time period. Not surprisingly, those Republican freshmen interviewed were uniformly supportive of the Boehner Rule. Many supporters cited the disadvantages of long-standing, powerful chairs. Sam Brownback (R-KS) argues that the Boehner Rule prevents the creation of fiefdoms, similar to those of past committee chairs.

I think the long-term implications of [the Boehner Rule] are you stop getting people matriculating into these positions of committee chairs and becoming dictators. How many years was Dan Rostenkowski chair of the

Tax Writing Committee for this nation? How many years was John Dingell in charge of Commerce? How many years was [Jack] Brooks in charge of Judiciary? . . . You've got to have some regular turnover or you're just gonna get people who accumulate fiefdoms.

Brownback's freshman colleague, Todd Tiahrt (R-KS), agreed, suggesting that long time committee chairs misuse the influence that accompanies these posts. He contends that a six-year limit on committee chair tenure will reduce the chances of corruption.

In the past, when we've had the former Judiciary chairman sticking in stuff for naming a building after himself, giving [his district] a million dollars for a crime school. That only comes about when you've been a committee chairman for a long amount of time. So, I think it's going to be less oriented towards power, you know, grasping power and holding on to power. And, I think it would be more responsive to people. I think it's gonna be positive for America in general, versus whoever happens to have the highest senior guy. Who can hold on to it the longest, you know? With power there does come a tendency for corruption—take advantage of the system. I don't think that will happen as much when you have a six year term limit. . . . So I think it's a very positive thing.

Tiahrt extends this argument beyond the confines of the institution to include district-level or constituency concerns as well. He contends that by adopting term limits for committee chairs, members will be less inclined to see Congress as a career, adopting the citizen legislator approach instead.

It gets away from being a career politician too. A guys comes in, he does what he can, then he goes back to society. And I think that's more what our founding fathers had in mind than what we have seen in the last 40 years. You get guys that come here at an early age and they die. And there's a tendency to get away from the district if you're not in touch with . . . I think it's just better because it's gonna move more towards a citizen legislature than it has been in the past. I see that as a positive.

Tiahrt was one of many junior Republicans to advocate committee and subcommittee chair term limits. In the minds of these members, chair term limits are a natural extension of House term limits and their desire for a citizen legislature in which all members have comparatively equal influence. Nathan Deal (R-GA), a second-term Republican who switched from the Democratic Party mid-way through the first session of the 104th

Congress, cited the need to include all members in the policy making
process, regardless of tenure.

> Frankly, had previous Congresses had term limits in place for committee
> chairmen, I think you would not have seen the overall eagerness for term
> limits for members of Congress come about. Because, many of the per-
> ceived problems with Congress come out of long standing committee
> chairmen who have had tremendous power because of their long tenure
> as a committee chairman of powerful committees. And, the perception of
> the public is that that power has been abused in many cases. So, I do
> support the idea of term limits for committee chairmen. I think it does open
> up the committee process a lot more. It gives an impetus, really, to having
> more people have an important role in the workings of the committee.

As Gimpel points out, the freshman Republicans are the strongest advocates of congressional limits (1996). Consequently, it should not be
surprising that they are also the greatest advocates of committee chair term
limits. Republican freshmen were not the only members to find fault with
strict seniority adherence in committee and subcommittee chair selection
however. Several junior to moderately senior Republicans, ranging from
four to eight years experience, echoed the freshmen's frustration with the
seniority system. Stephen Buyer (R-IN), a two-term Republican, argues
that "at some level, there's an equilibrium of knowledge and experience.
. . . Someone who has been here for eight years may not be any different
from somebody that's been here sixteen."

Conversely, very senior members, even senior Republicans, generally
objected to the Boehner Rule. Carlos Moorhead, the most senior Republican on two House committees, Judiciary and Commerce, was quick to
cite the benefits a seniority-based selection system.

> In this [job], you have to learn by your own mistakes instead of the mis-
> takes of others. I think the seniority system has, for the most part, worked
> very well.

Pat Roberts (R-KS), an eight-term Republican and Chair of the House
Committee on Agriculture, had more practical reasons for finding fault
with the Boehner Rule. Roberts worries that committee chair term limits
will force comparatively young politicians out of powerful posts in the
prime of their political career. Consequently, members will be less concerned about the work of the committee and more concerned about finding their next powerful post.

> Now say you have of the 13 major committees, [and] say you have a group of chairmen who are not particularly senior in years of service, but they are the chairmen. And, you have a six year window. That last four years ... you get to the jockeying of who's going to be chairman.

Roberts concerns were echoed by Norman Ornstein who argues that the internal incentives of House members are no longer tied to consistent, if unspectacular, committee work (1982). Instead, members are gradually looking toward external incentives that can only be attained through more outrageous behavior. Roberts' fear that members will be fighting over committee posts would likely illustrate this point.

Unlike the Republican Conference rule adopted in 1992, the Boehner Rule does not just apply to Republicans, it applies to either party, if they are the majority. Consequently, if the Democratic Party retakes majority control, the rule will apply to Democratic chairs as well. Several Democrats, senior and junior alike, argue the seniority rule works to insulate the members and prevent influence pedaling. David Bonior (D-MI), a 10-term Democrat and Minority Whip, contends that the seniority rule should be maintained because it safeguards the career aspirations of women and minorities.

> The seniority system is positive. The people who survive develop the skills to lead. The six-year limit the Republicans are putting on committee chairs is discriminatory because women and minorities will have trouble attaining chairmanships ... due to latent prejudices. [The seniority system] is more fair because it's blind to these prejudices.

David Obey (D-WI), a fourteen-term Democrat and ranking member of the House Committee on Appropriations, also cited concerns about the implementation of the Boehner Rule. He argues that a six-year limit on committee chairs would empower government agencies at the expense of House members by eliminating the persuasive power of a powerful chair.

> [The Boehner Rule is] a very bad idea because what it means is that bureaucracy is gonna await you. John Dingell is my best example. There are now five people in the Congress—that are in the House that know how to run a good oversight investigating operation. Dingell sure as hell is one of them. And he learned, I spent the Reagan years ... fighting OSHA when they were cutting deals that screwed working people and rewarded power brokers. Agencies, they will delay and delay and delay and delay information in following up. And, if you had a six year limit,

that just invites every damn agency to sit down and say: "Stuff them with paper and you could hold them up the first term because he's new. The second term he's beginning to know what he's doing, so he just has to be tougher. And by the third time everybody knows he's gonna be gone." I think it's a very dumb idea.

Obey's contention appears well founded. In *Congressional Committee Chairmen,* Andree Reeves argues that a powerful congressional committee chair, one molded by the institution, can dominate not only the committee but the bureaucratic structure as well (1993). Other congressional scholars also cite the organizational and institutional context of a chair's oversight power (Cooper and Brady 1981; Rohde and Shepsle 1987). Clearly, in this context, the implementation of the committee chair term limits would empower the bureaucracy at the expense of its oversight committee.

The interview findings suggest that the Boehner Rule creates more questions than it answers: What will be the legislative oversight effect of its implementation? Will it open the door to discriminatory selection procedures? Will it actually be implemented by the Republican Party? Will the Democratic Party reform the reform to eliminate the six-year restriction? Does it apply to committee leaders of a former majority party? Will a pseudo-seniority rule be implemented, whereby the next most-senior member replaces the departing chair?

Some of these questions can be answered in light of the 2001 election. At the beginning of the 107th Congress, several committee chairs were forced to relinquish their chairmanships due to the term limit restriction. In some cases this was a moot point, as members decided to retire instead of losing their committee posts. In fact, Commerce Chairman Thomas Bliley, one of the most influential members in the House, chose not to run for re-election. In addition to Representative Bliley, four other prominent chairmen stepped down in 2001. All of the retirees would have lost their chairmanship due to term limits. Departing members included Budget Chairman John Kasich (R-OH), Education and the Workforce Chairman Bill Goodling (R-PA), Ways and Means Chairman Bill Archer (R-TX), and Labor, Health and Human Services, and Education Appropriations Subcommittee Chairman John Porter (R-IL).

In general, member opinions toward the Boehner Rule were predictable. A term limit restriction on committee chair tenure was endorsed by junior members, regardless of party. Not surprisingly, senior members were less supportive. Boehner Rule advocates cite three advantages to the Boehner Rule: less mismanagement, better use of member expertise, and improved public image. Several members were cited by name as examples of mismanagement. Included in this list are Former Chair of the House Committee on Appropriations Dan Rostenkowski (D-IL), Former Chair of the House Committee on the Judiciary Jack Brooks (D-TX), and Former Chair of the House Committee on Commerce and current ranking member John Dingell (D-MI). Interestingly, on more than one occasion, senior Democrats celebrated the long and distinguished careers of both Brooks and Dingell.

While the Boehner Rule clearly changes the seniority rule, not enough evidence exists to predict what these changes will look like. It may effectively end seniority rule of congressional committees, but this seems unlikely. It also may be overturned by a new Democratic majority or the current Republican majority when the six years comes to pass. In short, congressional watchers will not know the full effect of this reform until it is fully implemented.

CHALLENGE #3: POLICY CAUCUSES

In addition to the Boehner Rule, other institutional changes associated with the 104th Congress have weakened or relaxed congressional norms. Both specialization and reciprocity are also under fire from the growth of broadly defined policy caucuses, which "operate outside the established structure of Congress" (Hammond 1997, 274).

One feature of the Republican reform package was the elimination of federal funding for such groups as the Congressional Black Caucus and Congressional Caucus for Women's Issues. Each of these is dominated by House Democrats, but even as these groups are being de-emphasized, other, Republican groups are taking their place. Junior members, especially freshmen, have formed a series of policy groups, called freshman caucuses, to better inform one another and maintain solidarity when contentious issues arise. In the past, groups like the Conservative Opportunity Society, formed by Newt Gingrich, succeeded in unifying Republican members in an effort to combat the aggressively partisan leadership tactics of former Speaker Jim Wright (D-TX) (Deering and Smith 1997). Freshmen of the 104th Congress utilized this model to create several policy groups, thus usurping the persuasive power of both the party and committee leaders.

Freshman Republican Tom Coburn (R-OK) is a member of several groups, including the Conservative Team and the Blue Dot Coalition, two conservative policy groups. Coburn explains the need for freshmen to remain united and outside the party's control. "We've got lots of leg-

still celebrated. Members still demand autonomy and predictability. As norms continue to survive, despite efforts at reform, they become more impermeable to those reforms (Hinckley 1988). In short, by not abolishing these norms, institutional reforms serve to re-enforce them. It will be interesting to see if the current challenges to the institution's traditions will produce a similar effect.

NOTE

1. Although Myers was not the most senior Republican on the committee, he was next in line to become chair. John McDade (R-PA), the most senior Republican on Appropriations, was under federal indictment, and thus unable to occupy committee or subcommittee leadership positions according to the Republican Conference rules. The Republican Party leadership, however, refused to endorse John Myers, despite seniority rule.

Chapter 5

PARTY SWITCHING IN AN INSTITUTIONALIZED CONGRESS

The sustainability of an institution's norms is directly related to the permanency and/or consistency of the environment (Matthews 1960). In the U.S. House, this environment is governed by the two major political parties, who manage the institution by a series of norms based on the partisan make-up of the membership. Given the stability of this majority/opposition tug-of-war, there is nothing that destabilizes the institution like a party switcher. Virtually every legislative rule, written or unwritten, spoken or unspoken, is situated within the party structure—from what bills are considered to what offices members occupy—political parties and their leaders set the rules and enforce them based on their membership. So when a member abandons a party to become an independent or switches to the other party, a sort of institutional chaos ensues. Rules are bent, norms are violated, deals are made, all in the hope of securing advantage or minimizing loss.

The irony of party switching is that while the act of switching is itself a violation of over 200 years of member conduct and party stability, the institution and the political parties have developed a series of informal guidelines to govern the party-switching process. Thus, even chaos can be managed in a consistent, predictable manner. This is yet another sign of a highly institutionalized body—one so stable and cohesive that anarchy itself must follow a series of carefully crafted norms.

The guidelines that party leaders follow when confronted with a party switcher pertain to three areas: the proper etiquette for encouraging a

potential party switcher to commit to the change, the new party's responsibility to reward the switcher with plum committee and/or subcommittee posts, as well as the new party's obligation to reconcile the needs
of their current members with those of the switcher. These norms play
out in a less than predictable way however. The party leadership may
view one switcher as more prized than another and work more diligently
to secure benefits for that member over others. Some switching members
may seek out the advantages inherent to such a move. Others will not.
Some switchers work with current party members to ease the transition
from one party to anther. Others will not. In other words, while the events
surrounding party switching may appear haphazard, the underlying principles are consistent and predictable. This makes them norms of party
switching.

THE CASE OF SENATOR JIM JEFFORDS

Party switching has a long, sporadic history in American politics. Only
a handful of House members and even a smaller number of Senators
have left their political parties in the past half century, making the past
50 years the most stable period (in terms of membership permanence)
in the 200-plus year history of Congress. Political parties have been and
continue to be integral to a member's electoral and substantive success,
so the decision to abandon one's party can be a difficult one. There are
times, however, when the member must weigh political and personal
upheaval of a switch against the electoral or political advantages that
might accompany it. If he or she concludes that a switch will best serve
his or her interests or those of his or her constituency, then a move is
possible and even attractive.

When Vermont Senator Jim Jeffords changed his identification from
Republican to Independent in May of 2001, thus shifting Senate control
from the Republican Party to the Democratic Party, he was the fourth
senator to switch parties while in office since the 1994 congressional
election and only the seventh senator to switch since 1953 (see Table
5.1). The Jeffords' case is an interesting one because it illuminates the
norms related to party conversions while at the same time demonstrating
the idiosyncratic nature of such events.

Most party switchers are junior members who have yet to attain a
leadership position in the chamber or the kind of personal or professional
recognition that more senior members enjoy. While it is true that Jeffords
was a junior senator from Vermont, as a third-term Republican, Jeffords
had risen to Chair of the Senate Committee on Health, Education, Labor,

and Pensions. This made Jeffords an extraordinarily important senator in the 107th Congress, considering President George W. Bush's assertion that his education initiative—the "No Child Left Behind Act"—would be the administration's first legislative objective. As it turned out, the Economic Growth and Tax Relief Reconciliation Act of 2001 (or Tax Cut legislation) would prove to be the focus of the president's first six months in office. Regardless, Senator Jeffords still occupied a prominent position in the Republican leadership.

Jeffords public comments concerning his decision to leave the Republican Party illustrate one of the first principles of a party switcher. Jeffords was on the ideological extreme of his party and felt isolated and ineffectual due to that marginalization. He was a liberal Republican, in the mold of the late Senator Nelson Rockefeller (R-NY) and more recently Senator John Chafee (R-RI), and thus out of step with the conservative wing of the party dominated by southerners and Midwestern Republicans. Jeffords came to believe that his power and status were being usurped by the conservative senate leadership, who, in the spring of 2001, attempted to rewrite the education bill without his input despite his leadership position in that policy area. In addition, news reports intimated that Jeffords was upset when President Bush chose not to invite him to an education event at the White House in which a Vermont teacher was being honored as national teacher of the year—a rather public display of discord between the White House and an influential party member. For his part, Jeffords suggested that the conflict over the education bill likely would have been the one of many between a liberal Republican, a conservative White House, and even more conservative Senate leadership.

> Increasingly, I find myself in disagreement with my party. I understand that many people are more conservative than I am, and they form the Republican Party. Given the changing nature of the national party, it has become a struggle for our leaders to deal with me, and for me to deal with them (Burlington Free Press, May, 25, 2001, Page 1).

One oddity of the Jeffords switch was that given the 50–50 deadlock in the Senate with a Republican in the White House, Jeffords had the choice of staying a Republican and remaining in the majority or switching and voting with the new majority party.[1] Given his electoral success in Vermont (in 2000, he was reelected as a Republican with 67 percent of the vote in one of the most Democratic states in the country) and Vermont's history of supporting independents—witness their U.S. House

Representative Bernard Sanders, the only independent in Congress prior
to Jeffords making the switch—Jeffords need not worry about his reelection hopes or the likely fallout from his constituents, most of whom
were Democrats or independents.

> I was not elected to this office to be something that I am not. This comes
> as no surprise to Vermonters, because independence is the Vermont way.
> My friends back home have supported and encouraged my independence
> even when they did not agree with my decisions. I appreciate the support
> they have shown when they have agreed with me, and their patience when
> they have not. I will ask for that support and patience again, which I
> understand will be difficult for a number of my friends (Ibid.).

A final important feature of the Jeffords switch concerns the deal he
made with the Senate Democratic leadership to become chair of the
Senate Committee on the Environment and Public Works. Prior to the
switch, Jeffords was chair of a similarly important policy committee,
Health, Education, Labor, and Pensions. The Senator possessed a long
history of progressive environmental positions and was considered an
important member of the Environment and Public Works Committee, so
his interest in that position was not surprising.

Deals are common when members switch parties, but they are less
common when a member moves from one party to become an independent. Again, the specifics of the Jeffords case allowed him this kind of
influence. With the Senate deadlocked at 50, Jeffords decision to leave
the Republican Party made the Democrats the majority party, regardless
of whether he joined the Democratic caucus or not. So, Jeffords was
able to stay an independent and be rewarded with a committee chair
post, an unprecedented event, but one in keeping with the norms of
party switching.

RECENT HISTORY OF PARTY SWITCHING IN THE U.S. CONGRESS

Jeffords is one of a small handful of U.S. Senate switchers in the last
half century. As Table 5.1 illustrates, only seven members since 1952
have left their elective party during their term in office. Of those, three
senators, Wayne Morse, Strom Thurmond, and Bob Smith, made multiple
moves, first to a non-partisan position or to a third party—Thurmond
was the first Independent Democratic elected to national office in 1954—
before rejoining one of the two major parties. In each case, the incentives
of being a member of one of the two major parties were very strong.

Table 5.1
Senate Party Switchers Since 1953

Senators	State	Year	Party Leaving	Party Joining
Jim Jeffords	Vermont	2001	Republican Party	Independent
Bob Smith	New Hampshire	1999	Independent	Republican Party
Bob Smith	New Hampshire	1999	Republican Party	Independent
Ben Nighthorse Campbell	Colorado	1995	Democratic Party	Republican Party
Richard Shelby	Alabama	1995	Democratic Party	Republican Party
Harry Byrd	Virginia	1971	Democratic Party	Independent
Strom Thurmond	South Carolina	1964	Democratic Party	Republican Party
Strom Thurmond	South Carolina	1956	Independent	Democratic Party
Wayne Morse	Oregon	1955	Independent	Democratic Party
Wayne Morse	Oregon	1953	Republican Party	Independent

Source: Adapted from U.S. Senate Document "Senators Who Changed Parties During Senate Service (Since 1890)."

Each of the senators listed in Table 5.1 maintained their seniority. In fact, many of them improved in ranking as a result of the switch. For instance, in 1964, when Strom Thurmond switched from the Democratic Party to the Republican Party, he went from seventh in seniority on the Senate Armed Services Committee to the third in seniority. Only Wayne Morse did not retain his positions on two prominent Senate committees, Labor and Armed Services, due largely to his insistence that his committee assignments be voted on by the Senate at large. In 1955, however, Morse switched to the Democratic Party, newly in the majority under the leadership of Senator Lyndon Johnson, and was rewarded with a coveted spot on the Foreign Relations Committee—he received retroactive seniority. Morse would later cast one of only two Senate votes against Lyndon Johnson's Gulf of Tonkin Resolution.

A more recent example, Senator Richard Shelby of Alabama, best illustrates the pattern of party switchers since the collapse of the once unified, Solid South. Like most of the House members who switched in the mid-1990s, Shelby was a conservative southern Democrat in a party dominated by northern or western liberals and with a constituency increasingly more inclined to vote Republican. So when the Republican Party won the House in 1994, several members of Congress, including Senator Shelby, took advantage of the opportunity to join the Republican Party. Among other committee changes, Senator Shelby went from the fifth ranking member on the Senate Banking Committee to the third ranking member. He also was added to the Senate Select Committee on

Intelligence, where he held the second ranking position and would later become the ranking Republican.

PARTY SWITCHING IN THE U.S. HOUSE OF REPRESENTATIVES

The politics involved in party switching in the U.S. House of Representatives are very similar to those in the Senate. In fact, the five southern Democrats who changed party affiliation in the months following the 1994 election faced circumstances mirroring those of Senator Shelby. Each was a conservative southern Democrat from the old Solid South— that region of the country dominated by Democrats as a result of the Civil War. Most faced increasingly difficult reelections, as the Republican Party gained a larger foothold in southern politics. Representative Nathan Deal, the first member to switch, was a conservative Democrat from Georgia. The Georgia congressional delegation had converted from entirely Democratic as late as the 1970s to one dominated by the Republican Party by the mid-1990s. In fact, when Representative Deal announced his intention to switch parties, long time Georgia Senator Sam Nunn was the only remaining white Georgia Democrat in the entire Georgia delegation. Representative Greg Laughlin of Texas faced comparable problems. He was a conservative Democrat from the oil-producing part of a state in the throws of a partisan realignment. The states of Mississippi and Louisiana were undergoing similar conversions as Representatives Parker, Tauzin, and Hayes were confronted with the option of switching.

As Table 5.2 suggests, from 1975 through 1995, 10 of 12 House switchers were southern Democrats abandoning the Solid South to join the Republican Party. Representatives Jarman of Oklahoma, Gramm of Texas, Ireland and Grant of Florida, and Robinson of Arkansas each made the decision to convert as their reelection margins narrowed and immediately preceding the realignment of their state delegations to majority Republican. The electoral turnover was very similar. With the exception of majority minority districts, the states of Oklahoma, Texas, and Florida are virtually devoid of the white conservative Democratic representatives so abundant only a few decades ago. Arkansas is one of the last holdouts from the Solid South. Each of the four members of the House delegation beginning the 107th Congress were white conservatives, one Republican, the other three Democratic.

Of the three most recent members to switch, only Virgil Goode of Virginia fits the southern conversion model. Goode, who was originally elected as a Democrat in 1996, ran unopposed in the majority agricultural

Table 5.2
House Party Switchers Since 1958

Members	State	Year	Party Leaving	Party Joining
Matthew Martinez	California	2000	Democratic Party	Republican Party
Virgil Goode	Virginia	2000	Democratic Party	Independent
Michael Forbes	New York	1999	Republican Party	Democratic Party
Jimmy Hayes	Louisiana	1995	Democratic Party	Republican Party
Mike Parker	Mississippi	1995	Democratic Party	Republican Party
Billy Tauzin	Louisiana	1995	Democratic Party	Republican Party
Greg Laughlin	Texas	1995	Democratic Party	Republican Party
Nathan Deal	Georgia	1995	Democratic Party	Republican Party
Tommy Robinson	Arkansas	1989	Democratic Party	Republican Party
Bill Grant	Florida	1989	Democratic Party	Republican Party
Andy Ireland	Florida	1984	Democratic Party	Republican Party
Phil Gramm	Texas	1983	Democratic Party	Republican Party
Eugene Atkinson	Pennsylvania	1981	Democratic Party	Republican Party
Bob Stump	Arizona	1981	Democratic Party	Republican Party
John Jarman	Oklahoma	1975	Democratic Party	Republican Party
Donald Riegle	Michigan	1973	Republican Party	Democratic Party
Ogden Reid	New York	1972	Republican Party	Democratic Party
Albert Watson	South Carolina	1965	Democratic Party	Republican Party
Vincent Dellay	New Jersey	1958	Republican Party	Democratic Party

Source: Compiled from Various Sources, including *Congressional Quarterly,* April 15, 1995, page 1085 and U.S. House Legislative Resource Center.

region of central Virginia in 1998 before leaving the Democratic Party in January of 2000. He won reelection in 2000 with 67 percent of the vote, facing only token opposition from an underfinanced Democratic opponent. His move away from the Democratic Party mirrored the state's evolution from a stalwart of the Solid South to its first Republican majority since reconstruction.

THREE FORCES DRIVING SWITCHES

Based on interviews with several House members, the motivation behind leaving one party and either joining another or becoming an independent falls into three general categories: The member's home district or state has realigned to favor the opposition party—or is likely to do so in the near future; the member is frustrated with the policy agenda and/or dominant ideology of his or her political party; and/or, the member has been approached with an attractive offer from the rival political party. These factors mirror the institution's norms when dealing with party switchers. While there are push factors, like constituency and mar-

ginalization, there are pull factors as well, in the form of attractive committee and subcommittee posts. In practice, these factors almost always
work together to persuade the member to make the switch.

Constituency Factors

The first of these falls outside the member's control.[2] Most congressional researchers agree that party dealignment, a movement by voters
away from identifying with a specific political party, has been ongoing
since the 1960s (Niemi and Weisberg, 1993). There is less of a consensus
about party realignment. This most likely arises from conflict over the
definition of realignment. Those that believe a long-term partisan realignment must convert one party from the minority to a majority, and in so
doing create the conditions for continued majority status, do not believe
that the southern conversion from a dominant Democratic region to a
dominant Republican region reflects a realignment. Instead, they argue
that this is a regional change that lacks the "decisive, unidirectional shift
. . . in partisan control over the agencies of government, as a new majority party appears at all levels and relegates its predecessor to the dust-
bin of history" (Ladd, 1991, 27). Under this definition, there have only
been three realignments in U.S. history.

Using a broader definition of partisan realignment, the conversion of
the South beginning in the late 1950s and still ongoing today is a regional
party realignment. In 1958, virtually every national elected official in the
Solid South was a representative of the Democratic Party. In 2001, every
southern state sent a Republican majority to the U.S. House of Representatives. In most cases, the only Democratic seats were held by African
American and Hispanic legislators from majority minority districts. For
instance, of the 11 members of the Georgia House delegation, only 3 are
Democrats—each of whom is African American.

In an important, symbolic way, the final vestiges of the Democratic
South ended in 1995 when five southern Democrats switched to the Republican Party. Only two of the five had serious constituency concerns.
The first was Nathan Deal of Georgia. Representative Deal was elected
with less than 60 percent of the vote in 1992 and won reelection with
58 percent in 1994—making his district a marginal one despite his incumbency (Mayhew 1974). Since 1996, Representative Deal has been
reelected as a Republican with progressively wider margins, as much as
75 percent to 25 percent in 2000.

The second party switcher, Representative Laughlin of Texas, was in
an even worse situation. He was a four-term Democrat in a marginal

district, who won reelection with only 56 percent of the vote in 1994. He represented Texas's 14th District—one of the largest oil-producing regions in the U.S.—a comparatively large district shaped like a triangle tucked between Houston, Austin, and San Antonio. He was also aware of a pending challenge from both political parties. From the Republican side, former 14th District Representative Ron Paul (who had switched from the Democratic to the Republican Party following his voluntary retirement in 1984), a popular five-term Congressman with substantial financial support from the oil industry, had already announced his candidacy. Within his own party, it was believed that Charles "Lefty" Morris, a local prominent attorney, would challenge Laughlin for the Democratic nomination. Consequently, Laughlin was faced with two alternatives: run for reelection as a centrist Democrat in a majority Republican district against a well-financed and popular Republican, or switch to the Republican Party and face the same opposition, only in the primary instead of the general election. Either way, he was doomed. Laughlin switched to the Republican Party and lost the primary election by a 54–46 margin. He blamed the Democratic leadership for the defeat, stating that poor committee assignments isolated conservative members on the ineffectual House Committee on Transportation and Infrastructure, making it difficult to be reelected.

> I was gonna switch regardless of the election. I think you'll find the other four guys will say the same. We'd been shut out. We'd been lied to by leadership. . . . After a while when you beat your brains out to get reelected and you're shut out of policy decisions, and people who have your philosophy are shut out as well. . . . It's difficult to represent your constituency when the leadership of the party shut you out.

Of the remaining three members who joined the Republican Party in 1995, only James "Jimmy" Hayes of Louisiana did not win reelection easily. Hayes was the last of the five to announce his switch and in doing so, he also announced his candidacy for an open Louisiana senate seat being vacated by the retirement of longtime Senator J. Bennett Johnston. Hayes went on to lose in the Republican primary. His House seat was won by a Republican with over 60 percent of the vote.

Ideological Differences with the Party Leadership

Like any organization, a political party has people of various political persuasions and ideological leanings. The difference is that in the U.S. Congress these viewpoints are fundamental to the success of the orga-

nization as well as the individual. Hence, the party leadership attempts
to keep members in line and voting for the party's position.

By the 1990s, life in the U.S. House of Representatives had become
a difficult one for southern Democrats. Both the party leadership as well
as many of the important committee leadership posts were occupied by
the more liberal wing of the party, ensuring that the conservative views
of many white southern Democrats were subjugated by the party majority.
In effect, they were getting it from both sides. On one hand, Republican
challengers were having more success supplanting Democrats throughout
the South. On the other, as their numbers dwindled they lost power and
influence, so the Democratic Party paid less and less attention to them,
isolating them on unimportant committees, and denying them leadership
positions. The ideological split is apparent in Table 5.3.

The scores for these five members are telling. In the two years of the
103rd congressional session, the southern Democrats' voting record was
anything but liberal, as witnessed by two prominent interest group scores.
The first, Americans for Democratic Action (ADA), was formed in 1947

Table 5.3
Interest Group, Presidential Support, and Party Unity Scores of 1995 Party Switchers

Party Switcher	Interest Group Scores		Presidential Support Scores		Party Unity Scores	
	ADA	ACU	Support	Opposition	Support	Opposition
Nathan Deal						
1994	15	67	63	36	61	36
1993	15	61	58	40	68	31
Greg Laughlin						
1994	50	60	68	21	64	22
1993	20	52	78	19	70	25
Billy Tauzin						
1994	15	76	54	42	50	47
1993	35	78	47	51	48	46
Mike Parker						
1994	20	67	64	31	59	36
1993	20	67	67	33	59	38
Jimmy Hayes						
1994	20	83	55	37	51	38
1993	20	70	65	28	65	30

Source: Compiled from Philip D. Duncan and Christine C. Lawrence, *Congressional Quarterly's Politics in America 1996: The 104th Congress,* various pages.

by several liberal Democrats, including Hubert. H. Humphrey and Eleanor Roosevelt, to advocate a liberal policy agenda and keep track of member voting records. None of the five Democrats scored over 50 for either 1993 or 1994. By contrast, none of the five were scored under 50 by the American Conservative Union (ACU), founded during the Barry Goldwater presidential campaign of 1964 to "mobilize resources of responsible conservative thought across the country and further the general cause of conservatism" (Duncan and Lawrence 1996, p. XIX). Thus, in terms of interest group assessment of political ideology, these members can only be described as conservative Democrats.

The presidential support scores are also striking. Presidential support scores are the cumulative tally of those congressional votes in which the president has an announced position prior to the vote. Given that 1993 was the first year of a new Democratic president after twelve years of Republican dominance in the executive branch, the House Democratic Party prioritized President Bill Clinton's legislative agenda. Even under these extraordinary circumstances however, the five Democrats could not manage a presidential support score of 80. In fact, during the first year of the 103rd Congress, Billy Tauzin sided with the Republican minority against the president more often than he did with the Democratic majority. Even President Clinton's most important initiatives were opposed by the southern Democrats. For example, none of the five voted in favor the Omnibus Budget Reconciliation Act—the President's 1993 budget—or the Family Medical Leave Act, the first major piece of legislation of the Clinton administration, the president having assumed office less than two weeks before.

The party unity scores also reflect the switchers' moderate voting records. Given their import to the goals of members, political parties are able to assert great influence over their members. The party whip and his or her deputies can secure deals, make threats, and twist arms in the effort to keep members voting the party line. Thus, party unity scores, the percentage of times a member votes with their political party where the majority of one party opposes the majority of the other party, usually average 80 percent or more. None of the five party switchers reached 70 percent for either 1993 or 1994. Again, Louisiana Representative Billy Tauzin voted with the Republican conference in party unity votes almost as often as he did with the Democratic majority.

A "Push" or "Pull" Factor?

While a partisan realignment (or change) in a member's constituency and an ideological conflict with the party leadership can serve as incen-

Nobody asks why all these guys are switching. Why do you think all the conservative Democrats are switching? They're switching because when the Democrats controlled this place it was controlled by liberal Democrats who locked them out of power and influence. And they never enjoyed abilities to move in positions of power. They never enjoyed that. So then when the Republicans took over, conservative Democrats were bastardized in the process by their own Democratic conference. It's very ugly how they get treated around here. And that's, you've had so many party switching. . . . Not since the Whig party have so many people switching. There are some very serious problems in the Democrat party today. Oh, within the conference itself. Very serious. And it happened because of 40 years of power and what that power did to decay a party. It's gonna take, it'll take them a few years.

Buyer's contention was supported by several Republicans who felt southerners were being stripped of their power to influence legislation. In her book, *The Seniority System in Congress,* Barbara Hinckley found that the vast majority of U.S. House committee chairs were southern Democrats because they entered the chamber at a young age and faced little, if any, token Republican opposition in their home districts. Hence, since the committee structure is based on seniority, southern Democrats eventually occupied the majority of the powerful positions (1971). The irony of southern realignment is that the South's reaction to liberal gains of the 1960s and 1970s was to gradually begin supporting Republicans, which meant that from 1970 to 1994, southern Democrats went from chairing virtually every important House committee to chairing no important House committees. This evolution was further exasperated by the fact that the less tenured southern Democrats found themselves serving on relatively unimportant committees, as the coveted assignments went to more liberal members. So even if they were able to get reelected enough times to become a committee chair, the committee they led would have little power anyway, certainly not enough to promote a conservative policy agenda.

Smith and Deering point out that only in the mid-1970s did the liberal wing of the Democratic Party finally assume control over the House Rules Committee, the committee that sets limits on debate and amendments for every piece of legislation (1997). The evolution away from southern control of House committees was furthered by the election of Tip O'Neill to be House Speaker in 1977. Another northern liberal, Thomas Foley of Washington, became Speaker in 1989 following the resignation of Texas Representative Jim Wright. Thus, by the 1990s, southern Democrats were not only losing chairmanships of important committees, they were being assigned lousy committee posts, which reduced their ability to influence important legislation.

With the exception of Tauzin, who possessed almost 10 more years of House experience than the next most senior party switcher, those who left the Democratic Party in 1995 were low-ranking members of the House Committee on Transportation and Infrastructure.[4] The Transportation and Infrastructure Committee, formerly known as the Public Works and Transportation Committee, is the quintessential consistency committee—"a committee with jurisdiction over programs that have concentrated benefits (for one's constituents) but widely dispersed costs" (1997, 75). Smith and Deering find that these committees have low national saliency, relatively high constituency saliency, and narrow jurisdiction (Ibid.). Thus, members of the Transportation Committee can use the position to promote local projects (and claim credit), which can help them to get reelected, but they have little or no ability to influence a wider policy agenda or gain national prominence.

The House Committee on Transportation and Infrastructure is a constituency committee, not one of the more attractive policy committees, where the ideological issues of the day are tackled, or a prestige committee attracting national or international media exposure and influence with fellow members. Given their prominence and high saliency both within and outside the chamber, House members tend to seek policy and prestige committees over constituency committees, once they have secured incumbent status (Ibid.). Representative Laughlin, who tried for years to obtain a different committee assignment, argued that the Democratic Party used committee posts as a way of cleansing the party.

> The House liberal leadership of our party stacked the conservatives from the South on this committee (Transportation) to put us in a closet. To put us away. We had no impact on policy. And some of us have been here six years and been trying to leave the committee for six years.

Conservative southern Democrats were unlikely to earn positions on the most attractive committees. Instead, if the highly-sought-after positions went to a Democrat from the South, those Democrats were African American members from majority minority districts.

Laughlin cites several examples, including one in 1993 when he was passed over for a Ways and Means opening. Following Democratic gains in the 1992 election, several positions were available on the most attractive policy committees and most influential prestige committees. Representative William Jefferson, a second-term African American Democrat

from Louisiana with a liberal voting record was offered a post on the
Ways and Means Committee when Laughlin, a third-term Democrat reelected with 72 percent of the vote, had, in his words, "earned right of
first refusal" based on his seniority. Representative Laughlin cites this as
evidence that the Democratic Party leadership promotes the interests of
southern Democrats from majority minority districts because they are
more liberal.

> You look at the Ways and Means committee assignments from the region
> that's made up of Georgia, Alabama, Tennessee, and Mississippi. . . . To-
> day the make-up for that region is Harold Ford from Memphis and John
> Lewis from Atlanta. Memphis and Atlanta are not reflective of that whole
> region. Those two representatives are reflective of the House Democratic
> liberal leadership. But you tell me that their districts are representative of
> the new south, the old south, or any south?

As Representative Laughlin asserts, one significant push factor relates to
the Democratic Party's willingness to isolate southern conservatives on
constituency committees and forward the interests of other members over
those of white southern Democrats.

Other institutional reasons made switching parties attractive, or created
pull factors, however. Most notably, as Democrats began inquiring about
switching parties, the Republican Party quietly offered switchers plum
committee posts, in many cases on the same committees that the Democratic Party rejected two years earlier. This was common knowledge
among members, for if the Republican Party wanted to encourage Democrats to switch, they would have to make it attractive for the member.
Commerce Committee Chair Thomas Bliley of Virginia put it simply, "I
never caught a fish on an empty hook."

That hook was a position on one of three committees, Appropriations,
Ways and Means, or Commerce. The House Commerce Committee is
one of the most influential policy committees in Congress, while both
Appropriations and Ways and Means are prestige committees, affording
members high visibility and influence. Representative Tim Roemer, a
Democrat and colleague of Louisiana Representative Jimmy Hayes when
they both served on the Science and Technology Committee, was con-
fident that Hayes had parlayed his move into an attractive committee
post. "I would suspect that Jimmy got a promise to be on the Ways and
Means committee. . . . So he cut a pretty good deal for himself to switch
parties."

For their part, four of the five party switchers reported that they asked for no special treatment, or deals, in order to make the switch. Representative Mike Parker of Mississippi recounted a conversation he had with Speaker Newt Gingrich prior to switching. "We're not gonna discuss committees." Parker told the Speaker. "We're not going to discuss seniority. We're not gonna discuss anything as far as deals. All I want to talk about is moving over and let you know that I'm gonna come." Upon officially switching to the Republican Party, Parker joined the Ways and Means Committee.

Only Representative Tauzin publicly admitted that he had worked with Speaker Gingrich and Commerce Committee Chairman Bliley to maintain his position on the Commerce Committee. The others stated that they were asked to submit a list to the Speaker of committees they would prefer. In each case, the members received their first or second choice. Around the chamber, however, member perception was that the southern Democrats would not have switched were it not for the improved committee posts.

Many members, even those not directly affected by the events surrounding the five members, were sympathetic to the constituency issues that helped bring it to fruition. Representative Jan Meyers, Chair of the House Committee on Small Business, links the constituency pressures of the switching member to their committee and subcommittee requests. In her mind, it is only logical that the Party work with the new member to help him or her be reelected and maintain the Republican advantage.

> Well, I think it's inevitable that if someone switches parties, for instance from Democrat to Republican after having run as a Democrat for a number of years, you are going to have to make some concessions to that individual. Not because he's done you a big favor. Because chances are he wouldn't be changing unless his constituency is changing. . . . [The switching member is] taking a risk when you make any major change in your policy stand, in your political party halfway through the game.

The risk of switching is significant but the benefits are considerable as well, especially for those members already marginalized by their own political party. The case of the five switchers in the 104th Congress illustrates the reasons members switch and the norms the party leadership follows when working with switching members. In short, the member must initiate contact with the opposition party and secure an appropriate arrangement with the new party.

APPEASING CURRENT MEMBERS

When Representative Nathan Deal and then Representative Greg Laughlin left the Democratic Party in the spring of 1995, the Republican Party leadership developed several guidelines, or norms, to both attract new members and appease current party members who might be upset by the process. First, switching members will be given their first or second choice of committees. Second, they will retain their seniority when swapping committee positions. Third, while retaining committee seniority, switching members will go to the bottom of their class within the committee. Finally, when a Republican is greatly harmed by the addition of a switching member, the Party leadership will work with the member to achieve an accommodation.

Committee work is incredibly important in the U.S. House of Representatives. The committees on which a member toils "determine the character of the member's career" (Smith and Deering 1997, 59). Most choose to specialize in a few specific policy areas, almost always these are associated with their committee assignments. For instance, a member's assignment to the Natural Resources Committee would take his or her legislative career in a much different direction than an assignment to the House Banking and Financial Services Committee. Thus, when a new member enters the House they may do more campaigning of the party leadership than they did getting elected, all in an effort to obtain the preferred committee post.

At the beginning of each new congressional session, the political parties must make committee assignments. Some years, this is a relatively easy process, as there is little turnover and few seats to fill. Other years, those with large freshman classes, the struggle to assign members can prove very contentious. Given the institutional importance of dispersed decision making, it is not that surprising that each party has a committee to make committee assignments. In *Congressmen in Committees,* Richard Fenno breaks down the practice of assigning members to committees and the process by which these decisions are made (1973). He finds that the selection process has guidelines but is often subjective. This subjectivity prompts Smith and Deering to suggest that committee assignments "can create ingrates and enemies just as easily as friends" (1997, 58).

This is also the case when switching members are added to the most attractive committees. One of the accommodations made to party switchers is that they not only move to a preferred committee, but they retain their committee seniority, thus bumping more senior committee members.

As Commerce Committee Chair Thomas Bliley put it, "if you're gonna encourage members from the other side to come across, you gotta treat them right." Thus, not only are members upset who were overlooked for committee posts, but so are committee members who lose seniority, not the least of which was one of Bliley's colleagues on the Commerce Committee.

Representative Michael Oxley, a conservative Republican from the cornfields of central Ohio's 4th congressional district, joined the Commerce Committee following a special election in 1981. From then until 1995, he went from the lowest-ranking committee member to Chair of the important Commerce, Trade, and Hazardous Materials Subcommittee and the committee's fourth ranking member overall. However, when Billy Tauzin switched to the Republican Party, he brought with him two more years of seniority on the Commerce Committee. This presented a difficult dilemma for the Republican leadership: aid the switching member by offering him a subcommittee chairmanship or risk losing the switcher by maintaining the current committee and subcommittee leadership hierarchy. There was no consensus among other members of the Republican caucus.

Republican Representative Scott Klug of Wisconsin, a third term conservative who was befriended by Oxley when he joined the caucus in 1991, suggested that the party leadership faced a difficult decision but that a member's loyalty to the party should be considered when considering subcommittee leadership positions.

> I think most [House Republicans] feel a sense of loyalty to Mike to say, "Look, you've been Republican much longer, a good member of the committee" not essentially penalize him in order to make Tauzin happy. And then you've got Tauzin who feels like he got some promises from the leadership in order to make the switch. . . . So it gets odd for individual members. But my sense in that case is what really matters is party loyalty and I think Oxley's been a good trouper for longer, and I think really, in that case, should get the break. Although our leadership I think is in an awkward position. Because if they don't deliver to Tauzin, then what can we dangle in the future for anybody else?

Several members, including virtually all of the senior Republicans interviewed, agreed that Tauzin should be rewarded for switching parties but that reward should not affect a current Republican's leadership position. Even a handful of the younger members, including those most closely identified with Speaker Gingrich, disagreed with giving Tauzin seniority. The difficulty of appeasing the current membership was illustrated by

Sam Brownback, freshman Republican from Kansas, who chided the
leadership for making deals with the switchers. "It makes some of us
think that maybe what we ought to do is switch to Democrats and switch
back to Republicans, and see if we get bumped [to better] committees."

One Republican who argued in favor of retaining Tauzin's seniority
was seven-term Indiana Republican Dan Burton, best known for his years
as chair of the House Government Reform and Oversight Committee and
its numerous investigations of President Bill Clinton. Burton took a more
pragmatic approach to the Tauzin/Oxley debate.

> I think we ought to try to encourage Democrats to come over if they are
> of our philosophy. . . . And in order to do that sometimes you have to
> make accommodations by saying, "Yeah, we'll give you a plum committee
> assignment or a chairmanship." So even though it might ace out one of
> our people, we need to look at the big picture, and that is continuing to
> hold power and redirecting the country. We want the country to go in a
> more conservative position, less government. It ain't gonna happen under
> those other guys.

Another party switcher, Mike Parker of Mississippi, defended Tauzin's
effort to acquire a subcommittee chairmanship. He argued that by seniority alone, Tauzin should be chair of the entire committee and not just
a subcommittee. "Billy Tauzin's got more seniority than Tom Bliley,
who's chairman of the committee. A lot of people don't realize that. So,
I mean, he just wanted his seniority. You know, he's been here 14 years,
whatever it is. That's what he wanted—that's only fair."

For his part, Representative Oxley agreed with the need to maintain
seniority when switching parties. Members rarely change parties when
that change will put them in the minority, Oxley pointed out, so power
and influence are the major factors behind the switch. Hence, a member
who chooses to switch would seek to maximize benefits related to that
switch.

> On the other hand, I personally think that that switcher ought to at least
> fit in the slot right behind the subcommittee chairs in the overall hierarchy.
> I think that when a person becomes senior enough to be a subcommittee
> chair then they ought to be recognized for that. And if somebody's switch-
> ing who has more seniority, I think we ought to recognize the fact that
> seniority's fine but it's also seniority in terms of party affiliation. And so
> as a compromise I've always thought that the best way to do it would be
> to fit that switcher into the scheme of things, either where he would go
> on normally or at the very least behind the existing subcommittee chairs.

Not surprisingly, Representative Tauzin had a somewhat different take on the situation. After years of acquiring seniority in the Democratic caucus, and battling the Democratic leadership, Tauzin felt he had deserved a leadership position on the Commerce Committee, because "seniority isn't earned in a party, it's earned in terms of years spent in the Congress. And that time entitles you to certain senior status among . . . your peers, regardless of what party you're in."

Tauzin was the only southern Democrat to admit making a deal with Speaker Gingrich before making the switch to the Republican Party. His status as a self-proclaimed good catch, provided him even more leverage than that of his southern Democratic cohort. The agreement Tauzin sought was that he be given full rights in the party if he won reelection as a Republican in 1996. According to the Congressman, however, it was Gingrich that insisted on giving him a leadership position in Commerce immediately.

> When I decided to make the switch, I informed the Speaker and he asked me about committees and stuff. I told him I didn't care this year, if I served in the low committees. But that, you know, eventually, if I was re-elected as a Republican I intend to have the full rights within the party. He insisted, he said, "You deserve it. You're entitled to serve on the committees that you serve on now. And we're gonna make it a simple 'walk-over'—same rank and position you would have been in seniority on the other side." And that's exactly what happened.

Six months after Tauzin switched the Republican Party, the leadership was able to broker a compromise between Oxley, Tauzin, and the other subcommittee chairs of the House Commerce Committee. Chairman Bliley asked the retiring chairman of the Telecommunications and Finance Subcommittee, Jack Fields of Texas, to split up his subcommittee. This began a series of changes that ended with the addition of one subcommittee and altered jurisdictions for the existing subcommittees. Tauzin was named chair of the newly created Subcommittee on Telecommunications, Trade and Consumer Protection. Oxley's subcommittee went from the Commerce, Trade, and Hazardous Materials to the Subcommittee on Finance and Hazardous Materials. To Representative Oxley's great frustration, Tauzin was given seniority over Oxley in the full committee, but remained behind Chairman Bliley, despite his additional term of experience in the committee. Both Representative Oxley and Representative Tauzin stated publicly their satisfaction for the arrangement. Oxley going so far as to report that the subcommittee component of the compromise had been his idea.

Not everyone was happy however. Two of the more ideological Republican freshmen termed it "business as usual." Another, Republican Representative Tom Coburn of Oklahoma, cited the compromise as yet another point against the seniority system. He argued that the conference should adopt a more democratic model for leadership selection, arguing that the committee or the conference should decide committee and subcommittee leadership positions.

> . . . To take and divide Telecommunications and Finance which should be together, and put Finance with Oxley's subcommittee is ridiculous. What it is is the same old good old boy system. How do we placate the ones that have been here a long time? What you should do is not placate either of them.

With the six-year committee chair term limit becoming reality in the 107th Congress, Commerce Chairman Bliley retired, leaving Representative Billy Tauzin as the most senior member of the committee and the next in line for the chairmanship. At the same time, Michael Oxley left the Commerce Committee to become chair of the newly formed House Committee on Financial Services, formerly known as the Banking Committee, a committee for which he was not even a member until he was appointed chairman. The speculation at the time was the new committee was created to end the long-standing feud between Oxley and Tauzin for the Commerce Committee Chairmanship. In effect, it was the final part of the deal between Oxley, Tauzin, and the party leadership. Only Congresswoman Marge Roukema, a 10-term New Jersey Republican, was upset with the decision to bring Oxley over from Commerce to Chair Finance Services. "I am gravely disappointed at the decision of the Steering Committee." She added, "however, I will be gracious and a good sport as a member of the Republican team" (http://business.cch.com/banking/news/financial%20services-pf,rn.htm). Roukema, long a thorn in the side of the Republican leadership due to her support for campaign finance reform, was the longest serving woman in the U.S. House when she announced her retirement November 8th of 2001.

CONCLUDING OBSERVATIONS

In an environment so dictated by political parties, the party switcher strikes at the heart of a highly institutionalized U.S. House of Representatives. Institutionalization is a function of predictability and nothing affects predictability like a member switching parties, committees, and subcommittees. Most every institutional function is situated within the party structure. So when a member abandons a party to become an independent or switches to the other party, the institutional chaos that erupts affects the way members view their party. Consequently, party leaders have developed a series of norms to govern the party-switching process. Members can rest assured that the party switcher will be handled in a predictable way that likely will not adversely affect their current position or institutional influence, except under the most exceptional circumstances.

The five conservative southern Democrats to leave the Party in 1995 were welcomed into the Republican caucus, which devised several rules to handle party switchers. Within reason, they gave the switchers their choice of committee posts. Switching members maintained their seniority, but were placed behind other members with the same seniority. Finally, the party worked with current members who were adversely affected by accommodations to switchers.

A more significant question, however, may be: why did these members feel they needed to leave the party to begin with? Clearly, there were constituency reasons for such a switch, as illustrated by the significant partisan changes throughout the South. There were also ideological differences between the members and party that led to a feeling of frustration for members seeking to change the prevailing view of the party.

More importantly, however, the members themselves say they did so because they felt marginalized. Their committee posts provided them little opportunity to affect policy, and even less chance to gain national or international exposure. The five members and other Republicans cited several reasons for the switch, most notably a feeling that they were being punished for being on the extreme of their party. These comments were not unlike those of moderate Republicans who argued that they were not considered, or even jumped for committee chairmanships because their ideology was not in keeping with the dominant ideology of the party. The evidence from Chapter 4 and that cited here suggests that both parties use committees as ways of isolating members with views outside the mainstream. In the case of the Democratic Party, they stick conservative Democrats on comparatively insignificant committee posts in an effort to marginalize their legislative influence. For the Republicans, moderate and non-conforming senior members not to the liking of the more conservative leadership are not allowed the chair committees for which they possess seniority.

NOTES

1. No matter what Jeffords did he would be voting with the majority. If he stayed a Republican, he would remain the majority. If he became a Democrat, the Democratic Party would have a 51–49 advantage in the Senate and would thus become the majority party. Finally, if he became an independent who voted with the Democratic Party, he would be voting with the majority. In this respect, no party switch has ever been as traumatic to the U.S. Congress as Jeffords switch. It changed the Senate leadership, committee chairs, subcommittee chairs, committee staff, etc.

2. Members may have some power to influence state party officials during redistricting cycles every 10 years, but altering congressional districts to maximize a party's dominance can be a contentious process that can backfire.

3. For almost a century, the Deep South voted almost exclusively for Democratic candidates in defiance of Abraham Lincoln and the Republican Party's insistence that the South remain part of the Union. The term Yellow Dog Democrat refers to the post Civil War assertion by many southerners that they would rather vote for a mangy yellow dog than for a Republican.

4. Tauzin himself admits that he only escaped this fate when as a freshman he was placed on the Democratic Committee on Committees and was able to influence his assignment to the Commerce Committee.

Chapter 6

STABILITY OF THE NORMS: 104TH CONGRESS

The discussion in Chapters 3, 4, and 5 illustrates a commonly held belief about the U.S. House. In addition to the gradual evolution apparent in any institution, the House undergoes sporadic periods of intense reform that often target formal as well as informal rules. In this chapter, another commonly held belief is discussed: that despite reform efforts, the House is a surprisingly stable institution. More specifically, the norms that guide member behavior are difficult to eliminate because they fulfill the members' need for a stable, predictable institution. Through two periods of intense congressional reforms, substantial member turnover, and increased external scrutiny, House members still rely on the institution's traditions. Thus, while reforms are adopted in order to change the institution, a centripetal force of sorts serves to maintain stability.

Students of Congress know very little about member attitudes toward norms. This is the case because scholars generally have not focused on them. The last studies to specifically ask members to discuss their attitudes toward norms were Herbert Asher's article "Freshman Representatives and the Learning of Voting Cues" (1973) and Matthews and Stimson's *Yeas and Nays: Normal Decision-Making in the U.S. House of Representatives* (1975). Prior to that, Matthews interviewed senators concerning their attitudes toward congressional norms (1960). Since the early and mid-1970s, however, the House has seen two periods of intense, sweeping reform and a majority party change. Consequently, our

current interpretation of congressional norms lacks an adequate understanding of member attitudes toward norms subsequent to these changes.

By interviewing the members themselves, two ends are achieved. First,
it fulfills the need for a preliminary exploration of the subject. Second,
this preliminary examination will suggest the existence of relationships
yet unstudied by congressional scholars. Again, Fenno's participant observation research provides the best blueprint for this method. Fenno
states that member interviews and observation, "are less likely to be used
to test an existing hypothesis than to formulate hypotheses for testing"
(1990, 57). Thus, this research should open the door to new and interesting ways of examining these relationships while at the same time
illustrating the stability of the institution.

MEMBER RESPONSES AND NORM INTERPRETATION

Chapter 3 demonstrates the effect that institutional dynamics can have
on its rules and guidelines. Other evidence, not dissimilar to that discussed in Chapter 3, has prompted some congressional scholars to claim
that the three norms tied to the committee system are all but dead (Moore
and Herrick 1995). Stephen Smith makes this argument in *Call to Order,*
suggesting that, since the 1970s reforms, junior members have stepped
outside the committee system in order to make policy, thus negating the
importance of the committee norms (1989). Others, like David Rohde
and Edward Schneier take a more pragmatic view, concluding, as Rohde
does that "behavioral patterns alone do not imply" a norm's existence or
nonexistence because they fail to address the member's expectation regarding the importance of these norms, which can only be garnered
through interviews (1988).

Norms are still important however, despite writings to the contrary.
So much so, that House members have widely differing, deeply felt attitudes toward these norms. A review of the findings suggests that certain
attitudinal patterns exist: junior members are generally less supportive
of seniority, specialization, and reciprocity, the three norms most closely
associated with the committee system. Conversely, senior members are
the most enthusiastic when discussing these norms. In each case, however, members were quick to acknowledge the lingering importance of
the committee-based norms and their direct or indirect effect on that
member's congressional existence.

Interestingly, the interviews suggest that an expectation of norm compliance still exists, thus contradicting some of the prevailing literature.

This expectation no longer appears to be defined by sanctions however. Rather, it is personal. The impetus to follow the informal rules is the member's hope to put himself or herself in the best position to retain or extend his or her influence.

SENIORITY

Herbert Asher's study of the learning process of freshman members examines this phenomenon by asking both freshman and senior members questions concerning congressional norms (1973). One of Asher's findings is that freshmen in the 91st Congress generally agree with most congressional norms. Asher goes so far as to argue that first termers are likely to agree with committee norms at a level comparable to that of their more senior colleagues. The findings discussed here differ greatly from Asher's. In interviews with 23 House members of varying party identification, philosophies, and experience, junior members consistently disagree with each of the three congressional norms discussed, suggesting that a generational phenomenon exists. The most glaring example of this trend concerns the seniority norm.

The term seniority norm refers to the distribution of influence based on deference and respect for length of continuous service to both the party and the institution. The primary importance of member seniority concerns its relationship to the power and influence, namely that accumulated by continuous service to a committee or subcommittee and the eventual ascension to chair. As Representative Pat Roberts (R-KS), former Chair of House Committee on Agriculture suggests:

> [Chairmanship] gives you, if not complete control, almost complete control. You set the agenda. You decide what, when, and how bills are considered. . . . You decide who serves on senior staff. You pretty much guide the committee in the legislative direction that you want to achieve. In short, you're the lead dog.

Initially, committee chairs were conceived merely as agents or moderators of congressional committees (Cooper 1970). By the 5th Congress, however, several House chairs dominated their committees, deciding the time and place of committee hearings, choosing witnesses, and stalling legislation regardless of congressional sentiment (Smith and Deering 1990). When political parties took over the operation of committees in 1846, committee chairs, selected via disparate criteria including member

tenure, had solidified their position as the dominant actors in the committee system (*CQWR,* January 24, 1987, p. 140).

The long-standing relationship between committee chairs and institutional influence may be best characterized by Woodrow Wilson, who
argued that the American system was "government by the chairmen of
the Standing Committees of Congress" (1885). This power is magnified
by the influence that committee and subcommittee chairs have on
constituency-benefit projects. More recent congressional scholarship supports this claim (Fenno 1973; Deering and Smith 1997). In an article
entitled *A Dead Senator Tells No Lies: Seniority and the Distribution of
Federal Benefits,* Brian Roberts argues that the distribution of federal
benefits as an effort to promote constituent interests is a power possessed
by committee chairs (1990). In fact, Roberts argues that with the substantial public exposure and prestige that accompany committee and subcommittee chairmanships, these positions become remarkably attractive
to members regardless of tenure. New members, however, enter the institution's seniority hierarchy at the bottom of what Roger Davidson and
Walter Oleszek termed "the internal career ladders that they could ascend
through uninterrupted service" (1994). Thus, these members have reason
to view seniority as a barrier to power and prestige afforded only those
in senior positions.

This relationship became apparent while doing the interviews. Junior
members consistently disagreed with a system whereby members are
afforded influence and prestige based on the length of their continuous
service. While most junior members simply disputed the idea that experience should or does equate to influence, the freshman members interviewed made this case most forcefully, arguing that a seniority-based
committee system stifles members with real-life experience. Freshman
Republican Tom Coburn (R-OK) minced few words.

> I think seniority is a stupid system. What you want to try to do is match
> talents and backgrounds with jobs and positions. Because you've been
> here doesn't mean you're a great leader, [It] doesn't mean you're a great
> committee chairman, [It] doesn't mean you have great negotiating powers.
> What it means is you have a great ability to get reelected.

The belligerent nature of Coburn's comments accurately illustrates the
general dissatisfaction freshmen have with a seniority-based committee
system. This discontent was primarily directed at the Democratic model
of seniority compliance and, specifically, those Democratic committee
chairs who use their powers to subjugate the minority. Other Republicans

were less critical of the seniority system than of the 40 years of continuous Democratic committee control. Stephen Buyer (R-IN), a second-
term Republican, discussed his first term in office. He argues that being
a junior Republican in a Democratic Congress made his committee work
unpleasant.

> I have problems with the seniority system when I experience . . . a system
> within the institution that had become arrogant, closed, mismanaged and
> undemocratic. And I don't care which party's in control, when you have
> one party in control for 40 years, that's what happens. That was the result.
> And so you had committee chairmen who had chaired committees for a
> very long time, who were very arrogant. And who were, not only were
> they stale in their ideas, but very closed. It did not make for a pleasant
> place to go to work. So, I mean, that caused real problems with the se-
> niority system.

Buyer's suggestion that committees were "mismanaged and undemo-
cratic" under Democratic leadership was a common assessment by junior
Republicans. Most cited the need for committee chair term limits and
the adoption of the Boehner Rule.

Another reason for committee chair rotation cited by House members
concerned the chair's competence. As discussed in Chapter 4, several
junior and moderately senior members advocate term limits on committee chairs because some senior members are not necessarily the best
qualified to run the committee. Scott Klug (R-WI), a third-term Republican from Madison, Wisconsin, contends that a seniority rule promotes
one attribute of a member, when several attributes, aside from length of
tenure, should be considered.

> In some cases, the folks who [are] most senior clearly [are] not the most
> capable. And, [Congress] should be operated, in my mind, like a business,
> where you want the best people in charge. It shouldn't be operated like a
> university with tenured faculty, and . . . length of service doesn't neces-
> sarily define qualification.

By contrast, senior Republicans, especially committee chairs, generally endorsed the seniority system. They did so by turning around the
arguments made by the junior members. Where junior Republicans argue
that qualifications should extend beyond the institution, senior Republicans contend that without institutional experience, relevant external experience is squandered.

Among the senior Republicans, an interesting dichotomy appeared between those who supported the seniority system for practical reasons and those worried about the fairness of other selection methods. Senior Republicans who cite practical concerns contend that senior members are more knowledgeable and more realistic about the policy process than members with less seniority. These traits make length of tenure an important attribute for committee leadership. John Myers (R-IN), a 15-term Republican who was bypassed for the chair of the House Committee on Appropriations, analogized work in Congress with that of being a lawyer or doctor.

> It means experience. This morning I had about three different agencies in here. And the value of experience is the fact that I know the agencies, and I know that what they tell us, I know whether it's true or not. Unfortunately we are [deceived] sometimes. But, that's the value of experience. . . . I've talked to many attorneys who, I said, "Aren't you a better attorney today than you were when you first got out of law school?" "Sure." Physicians. I had a number of physicians in yesterday, and I asked them the same question. And, of course, it's experience. My wife has had several cancers, and when she was first discovered with cancer six years ago, we didn't look for someone just out of medical school, we looked for someone who had seen cancer before, who hopefully successfully treated cancer, because that experience is so valuable. The same is true here in the committee system.

Mike Oxley (R-OH), an eight-term Republican and Chair of the Commerce, Trade, and Hazardous Materials Subcommittee of the House Committee on Commerce, also finds the practical value of experience. He explains that members are influenced by wisdom that can only come through sustained work in the institution. "A colleague of mine told me on the floor a few minutes ago, he said, 'The longer I'm here the more the seniority system looks good.' There's a lot of truth to that," he explained.

In discussing the practical advantages of attaining seniority, Oxley maintains that the senior House members are more knowledgeable in a given area. Consequently, he respects the judgement of his senior colleagues when contentious legislation is under consideration.

> No question about it. I think that the beauty of the committee system in any legislative body is the ability to concentrate one's focus on particular issues that you become reasonably expert in those areas. And so you do tend to show deference to members who are recognized as A- having seniority and B- having some knowledge in a particular area, which gen-

erally reflects around as committee assignment. And so I see a lot of that. I do that myself with members on other committees that I have respect for and know that they've been there and know what they've been through and know that they understand the issue far greater than I. So yeah, I think that's very important.

Oxley was not the only member to insist that experience is imperative to fully understand the policy-making process. Like Myers and Oxley before him, Dan Burton (R-IN), a seven-term Republican and Chair of the Western Hemisphere Subcommittee of the House Committee on International Relations, cites the practical reasons for promoting members with experience. Burton contends that becoming a committee or subcommittee leader necessitates both an understanding of the institution and the people who work there.

I think that there is merit in having a seniority system, after having been here awhile—Not because I'm one of the more senior members, but because it's hard to understand and learn all the rules and regulations of the House. . . . It takes a little time to learn the people that you have to work with.

Burton is quick to add, however, that the very things that make a member's experience positive also allow members to misuse their influence and give the seniority system a bad name.

Now, there's also some things wrong with it. And the things that are wrong with it is, it gets people entrenched in there for long periods of time who become tyrants. I used to call, when I was always taking on the College of Cardinals, we call them, in the Appropriations committee, I would go down there and these guys were entrenched, you couldn't get them out. And, I'd have to go down there and fight them hammer and tong. I'd be trying to cut spending by introducing amendment after amendment after amendment. I became a real thorn in their side over a period of about three years. They'd go nuts every time I came to the floor. And even though I had fought valiantly, I was successful on relatively few occasions—maybe, out of a hundred amendments, I'd get 10 or nine. And, it's because they have such power.

Each of the three previous members, Myers, Oxley, and Burton, cited practical reasons to value senior members and promote them to committee leadership positions. Three other senior Republicans agreed that a seniority-based committee system is preferable to other systems, but their argument concerns the fairness of other selection methods. Thomas

Bliley (R-VA), an eight-term Republican and Chair of the House Committee on Commerce, contends that seniority is the fairest way to select committee and subcommittee chairs because it removes the party from the selection process.

> Well, I saw what Winston Churchill said about democracy: "It's a lousy form of government. [But], until somebody comes along with a better one, it's the best we have." [The seniority system] is good. I'll tell you why. When you go the other way in which you have, based totally on election as to whether you will be . . . a subcommittee chair or a full committee chair, the dominant wing of the caucus, in that case, in the Republican caucus, the conservative wing will [win]. The Democrats, . . . their liberal wing that dominates.

Interestingly, Bliley was one of three Republicans to be promoted to chair over more senior colleagues on their committees. Despite this fact, Bliley still supports a seniority-based committee chair selection process. Bliley's fears concerning the party are directed both at internal and external forces within the party. It appears that the fear of party interference is not confined to ideological shifts. Instead, it is directed at two forces: tyranny of the majority or tyranny of the minority. Bliley's argument demonstrates his concern that a majority of a party would grasp control of the important committee and subcommittee posts and the leadership positions to make these committee selections.

Pat Roberts (R-KS), an eight-term Republican and Chair of the House Committee on Agriculture, was more fearful of the ideological dogma of a powerful Speaker or small group of party leaders using the power of committee leadership selection as patronage. Roberts argues that the seniority system protects the institution from a tyranny of the minority.

> In general, the seniority system is much criticized in the public and in the press and probably by members who are not senior. But, it's probably way ahead of whatever's in second place in regards to a fair way to determine leadership. If you go back and take a look at reform under the days of Joe Cannon. . . . the good old boy system and your larger states and the people that had the power at that particular time were handing out your subcommittee assignments and your committee assignments. Sort of a smoke-filled room kind of a situation. Seniority at least gets you out of that.

Bob Livingston (R-LA), a 10-term Republican and Chair of the House Committee on Appropriations, extends the fairness arguments of both

Bliley and Roberts to include the size of larger-state delegations. Livingston, one of the three members to bypass a member of greater committee seniority in the 104th Congress, maintains that if committee and subcommittee chairs were elected by a democratic vote, without deference to seniority, states with large delegations would stack the important committee and subcommittee leadership posts.

> [Without a seniority system], the leadership positions, chairman of Appropriations, Ways and Means, Rules, plus all of the other elected leadership positions would presumably go to states like Texas, California, Florida, New York, maybe some of the bigger Midwestern states. They sure wouldn't go to a state like Louisiana with only seven members. Small states would be left out of the works.

As the data suggest, Republican legislators are in two camps. Junior Republicans argue that the seniority system values only one member attribute, seniority, and disregards other important factors like practical experience and ability. In contrast, senior Republicans contend that institutional experience should be valued over pre-legislative experience and committee leadership selection should be left to forces outside the parties' control. A less-direct implication of the senior Republican comments was that their junior colleagues fail to understand the importance of seniority until they themselves are senior.

House Democrats were generally supportive of seniority-based committee leadership selection. One exception to this trend was Tim Roemer (D-IN), a five-term Democrat and Ranking Member of the Energy and Environment Subcommittee of the House Committee on Science. Roemer argues that the junior Republicans are correct to criticize the seniority system for discounting practical experience. His view of the seniority rule's future, however, appears somewhat different. Roemer argues that experience remains important, but it should be only one factor in a complicated decision matrix.

> I do not think that we should just keep a system intact that merely rewards people based upon the amount of time they serve in Congress. I think that your ability to take on such potentially powerful and esteemed positions as ranking chairs and chairmanships should depend on a host of factors. It should depend upon time, it should depend upon expertise developed that has direct relevance to the issues within the jurisdiction of that committee. It should be based upon your interest in those issues before the committee. And it should be based upon the time you spend in that committee. And all those factors add up to, I think, not just a powerful and

respected ranking member or chairman, but an effective ranking member
or chairman.

Roemer's argument appears directed at the interest and competence of a
few senior colleagues, suggesting that senior members are not necessarily
the most attentive to the issues under consideration.

> We have some people on our committees, on the committees that I've
> served on, Education and Science, that rarely show up, that are still in the
> top seven or eight, nine people in terms of positions of power. Yet, when
> we have some mark ups and we have some committee hearings, they're
> nowhere to be found. And, that does not sit well with some members
> within the caucus and within the committee. It also does not bode well
> that when you are authoring and drafting legislation, the hearings help you
> develop an expertise, and they help you be able to contribute new ideas
> to a mark up of a piece of legislation based upon what you've heard from
> witnesses, from the department, from agencies, from the grass-roots, from
> your home state. It also lends to a very bipartisan atmosphere, where you
> work together with another member. If you are rarely there for hearings
> and mark ups, you're not gonna be able to develop some of the same
> working relationships.

Roemer seemed quite agitated while discussing the attentiveness of
his more senior committee colleagues. In fact, he maintains that the three
Republican seniority violations prior to the 104th Congress were "acutely
savvy moves" by Speaker Gingrich because they bring "new visions and
new ideas" to the party. Although he is not optimistic, Roemer is hopeful
that the Democratic leadership will take similar action, when the opportunity arises.

> I would hope that if Dick Gephardt were elected Speaker of our party that
> he would use some of the same powers that Speaker Gingrich has used
> to get some new faces and some new people into the different positions
> of power within the committee structure. One of the problems with the
> Democratic party through the course of the last 20 years has been that
> there have been very few challenges and very few successful challenges
> to the committee system.

Aside from Roemer, however, each of the Democrats interviewed
voiced enthusiastic support for the seniority system. Bob Clement (D-TN),
a five-term Democrat and Ranking Member of the Coast Guard and
Maritime Transportation Subcommittee of the House Committee on Transportation, agreed with Roemer that some members should not be com-

mittee chairs, but he endorsed the seniority system as a primary basis for committee leadership selection.

> I think the longer you're here, the more effective you can be, if you apply yourself. But, it really comes down to the individual too, because we've got some lazy members, and then we have some that are energetic. I give examples of John Dingell, a prime example of that. He's still like a kid in a toy store. I mean, he's as excited today as he was the first day he arrived.

Interestingly, Clement's endorsement of John Dingell (D-MI), a 20-term Democrat and Ranking Member of the House Committee on Commerce, conflicted drastically with the comments of many Republican members who cited Dingell as an example of the need for committee chair term limits. As Republican comments in Chapter 4 illustrate, members of different parties are noticeably split on the effectiveness of John Dingell. Democrats are enthusiastically supportive, while Republicans are uniformly critical. In *The Contemporary Congress,* Burdett Loomis discusses the case of former House Committee on Commerce Chair John Dingell (D-MI) (1996). Several Republican members cite Dingell as a primary example of an arrogant committee chair who no longer serves the committee as much as he serves his own interests. Using the example of a contentious air quality bill under consideration in the 1980s, Loomis finds that Dingell is an incredibly effective chair, managing not only the egos within his committee but vocal opponents in the party as well (1996). Thus, Republican dissatisfaction with Dingell, and other powerful former committee chairs like Dan Rostenkowski (D-IL), and Jack Brooks (D-TX) may have more to do with their legislative effectiveness as less to do with the belief that these committees are mismanaged.

Interviews with three senior Democrats produced predictable comments. Each agreed that experience should be the primary basis for committee leadership selection. David Obey (D-WI), a 14-term Democrat and Ranking Member of the House Committee on Appropriations, argues that the primary method of selection for committee chairs should be seniority, but exceptions are occasionally necessary.

> Seniority is a decent system, provided you are willing to use it safely. . . .
> The seat that you hold comes from your district. The chairmanship that you hold comes from the caucus. You have to be able to meet your responsibility to the caucus as chairman. The caucus has a responsibility to find somebody who can. So, I think unless you're comfortable with the idea of members bidding for chairmanships on the basis of passing out

campaign contributions to each other and things like that, seniority is as
good a device as any in order to sort out how ambitious people allocate
[power]. But, you have to be prepared to break it to have someone who
obviously doesn't have the leadership qualities, or somebody who doesn't
have the health or the integrity to run the show.

It is not a coincidence that Obey mentions health concerns as an important factor in the selection process. Obey became Chair of the House
Committee on Appropriations when William Natcher (D-KY) fell ill
during the 103rd Congress. After the 1992 elections, Obey challenged
Natcher for the chairmanship but redrew his challenge before the vote.
Later, when Natcher was unable to carry on his duties as chair, Obey
was elected chair by a conference vote.

> I did challenge Bill. I had been urged to challenge him when he ran two
> years earlier, and it was obvious to me that there was no need to do that
> because Bill was in good shape then, and also I didn't think that I would
> stand a prayer of toppling somebody who was as liked and respected as
> he was. But when it became obvious he couldn't handle committee [lead-
> ership], I felt there was a very big difference between the energy level
> and the drive that Bill would bring versus [myself].

David Bonior (D-MI), a 10-term Democrat and Minority Party Whip,
was reticent to discuss the details of any particular seniority rule violation, however, he did mention the party's desire to standardize the selection process when possible. With only extreme exceptions, Bonior
argues that the seniority is the appropriate basis by which to make committee leadership decisions because member turnover demands consistency in important positions.

> The large turnover of the recent years illustrates the importance of se-
> niority. You need consistency at the top, and the seniority system assures
> this despite the changing membership.

Lee Hamilton (D-IN), a 16-term Democrat and Ranking Member of
the House Committee on International Relations, had more practical reasons for advocating member seniority when selecting committee leaders.
Similar to the concerns of senior Republicans Thomas Bliley and Pat
Roberts who fear party influence, Hamilton argues that the seniority system insulates Congress from external influences and opens the process
to women and minorities.

When you take away seniority as an organizing principle, you cede the advantage to the Executive Branch. They could more easily influence committees and, as a consequence, public policy. On top of that, those members from small states, women, minorities, [etc.] . . . may have difficulty rising to a committee chairmanship [because] they can't get the votes in the conference.

Representative Hamilton's argument concerning members of small state delegations, women, and minorities running for committee chairs illustrates the dilemma faced by Bernard Sanders (I-VT), a third-term independent. Sanders is the at-large representative of Vermont and the only independent currently serving in Congress. Under an unwritten agreement with the Democratic Party, Sanders is able to ascend the ladder of committee seniority as a Democrat. Without the seniority system, however, few, if any, members would support his candidacy for a given committee or subcommittee leadership position. In fact, under the scenario described by Hamilton, committee and subcommittee chairs would be elected by a party caucus or conference vote. Hamilton, like Bob Livingston before him, suggests that this process would be dominated by populous states with large party delegations. The implication is that states like California, New York, and Texas would dominate the leadership positions on the primary House committees, should the seniority system be totally abandoned. With no other House members in the Vermont state delegation, coupled with his independent party status, Sanders could expect very little, if any, support in an effort to secure a position on a important committee. Not surprisingly, Sanders voices strong support for the seniority norm based on this reason.

In my instance, the only independent in Congress, I had to reach an agreement with the Democratic leadership to even get [an assignment] to begin with. Now, I am treated as if I am Democratic, and . . . I move up the ranks in terms of seniority. . . . Without the seniority system, I would have no chance at being a chair. So, for me personally, it works quite well.

A predictable but interesting dichotomy of opinions became apparent between junior and senior member attitudes toward the seniority norm and the seniority rule that arose in the committee system. Every junior member interviewed spoke against a committee leadership selection method that elevates a member's continuous service over other attributes. Junior members insist that competence and practical experience should be taken into account when selecting committee and subcommittee leaders. One explanation for junior member dissatisfaction with the seniority system concerns the distribution of institutional benefits, which obviously subjugates freshman members. There is another explanation however. It is possible that the members of the 104th congressional class lack a careerist agenda for which the institution is designed. Thus, freshmen may find fault with the seniority system for policy reasons over a preoccupation with their career motives.

With only one notable exception, senior members consistently favored the seniority system. The arguments in favor of seniority were more varied than those against. Senior members argued that there were practical as well as fairness reasons for maintaining the seniority system. The practical reasons include the importance of institutional experience that familiarizes one with both the policy process and the people involved. The fairness reasons pertain to both internal and external threats. Committee leaders from both parties argue that the seniority system staves off the threat of party dominance as well as encroaching external influence while ensuring that women and minorities have an equal opportunity to rise to committee leadership.

Much of the apprehension concerning the elimination of a seniority-based selection system is discussed by congressional watchers as well. Schneier finds that members believe in the practical reasons for continuing the seniority system (1988). Specifically, he argues that members rely on the knowledge and experience of committee chairs. Thus, the day-to-day operation of the House would suffer as a result of a different selection system. Hinckley maintains that larger, theoretical concerns make the seniority system an attractive institutional feature. In short, she contends that the seniority system protects members. It protects them from interest groups, from political parties, from the president and the executive branch, but most importantly, the seniority system protects members from themselves by eliminating the inevitable competition that would arise with any other system (1971).

SPECIALIZATION

Most House members serve on one or more committees and three to five subcommittees. These committee and subcommittee assignments greatly influence a member's legislative fortunes (Copeland 1987; Munger 1988). A number of studies have established the importance of committees and subcommittees in the legislative process (Fenno 1973; Deering and Smith 1997). For the members themselves, committee assignments become similarly important because they are the basis for policy-making influence (Bullock 1973; Shepsle 1978; Deering 1996).

New members and those hoping to move to other committees spend the weeks following the election campaigning for good committee posts. Each party impanels a committee of hand-selected senior members and party leaders who evaluate member requests. Democratic members serve on the House Steering and Policy Committee while the Republicans employ the Committee on Committees. Given the importance of committee assignments, the selection process itself is quite difficult. Members submit a list of their preferred committee assignments, and the party leadership attempts to place them on the committees they request. Bob Clement, a former member of the House Steering and Policy Committee that makes committee assignments for Democrats, discussed the effort to please members.

> When I was here for the first year, Speaker of the House Jim Wright appointed me to the Steering committee, Steering and Policy committee on the Democratic side, where I worked with all the members, and particularly the new freshman class, on appointments. And I tried my best to get the committee appointments that they so desired for the freshmen, realizing that it would be very difficult to get on certain committees, such as Ways and Means, Commerce, and Appropriations, would be more difficult. Therefore, we had them put down their first, second, and third choices. And practically everyone got either their first or second choice.

When they are assigned to committees that correspond to their interests and experience, members quickly find their niche, and begin the process of becoming specialized (Matthews and Stimson 1975). Occasionally, however, a member is assigned to a committee and subcommittees that have little or no relevance to that member's background or personal inclinations, much less his or her constituents. In this event, they either attempt to move from those committees as soon as possible (Bullock 1973) or they may choose to focus their energy on one or two specific committee or subcommittee areas which most closely match their own interests (Shepsle 1988). In either event, the areas a member finally settles on become his or her areas of specialization.

The member interviews substantiated much of the previous research, namely that most House members specialize (Matthews 1960; Peabody 1976; Matthews and Stimson 1975; Hinckley 1988; Uslaner 1993). The reasons for specializing were less uniform however. Moderately senior members generally argued that specialization is a way of parlaying one's committee and subcommittee assignment into a position of influence, thus mirroring congressional scholars' perceptions of the specialization norm (Hinckley 1988; Smith 1989). Those members with less experience, however, especially those freshmen interviewed, put much less faith in specialization.

Whether by circumstance or preference, several junior members claimed to be generalists. In some cases, these members were assigned to mark-edly unrelated committees or subcommittees, so the generalist claim was one of necessity over choice. Bullock would argue that over the next one to three elections, these members will lobby to move to more appropriate committee assignments (1973). Other freshmen voiced opposition to the idea of specialization because it encourages members to trade votes and rely on the knowledge and expertise of other, more experienced, House members. For instance, Representative Buyer contends that specialization keeps members from becoming involved in issues outside their commit-tee work. "I'm more of a generalist," he explains when discussing the importance of representing his district no matter what the issue. Given his practical experience as a prosecutor in the U.S. Attorney's Office and a Gulf War veteran, however, Buyer's committee and subcommittee as-signments match his interests.

> The interesting thing is that Congress is kind of a make-up of society. It's hard to imagine that, but it really is. And the committee system, one of the nice things is how individual members are chosen to sit on certain committees. It deals with your background. And, you know, I've been a prosecutor in the U.S. Attorney's Office and a veteran, and I'm still a Major in the Army Reserves. I mean, what I do is a perfect fit. Right? Veterans' Affairs and National Security and Judiciary subcommittee on Crime. It's a perfect fit. America gets everything out of me.

Even though he considers himself a generalist, Buyer's committee and subcommittee work would suggest that he is particularly interested in issues directly or tangentially related to the issues faced by his commit-tees and subcommittees. Other Republicans admitted generalist tenden-cies; however, these appear to be a product of circumstance instead of a personal inclination. Representative Coburn argues that committee and subcommittee assignments dictate that they become competent in several unrelated areas of congressional action, thus spreading his influence into several legislative areas.

> If you look at the three subcommittees that I'm on, I'm not specialized at all. I deal with all health issues in this country, all environmental issues in this country. I deal with all telecommunications, I deal with all finance, and I deal with all energy and all power. . . . I cover a broad area. I work

aggressively in lots of areas, behind the scenes and through the Freshmen Caucus to get a lot of stuff done.

Coburn's allusion to the Freshmen Caucus provides some insight into his beliefs concerning specialization. As discussed in Chapter 4, broad policy groups like the Freshmen Caucus usurp the specialization norm by pooling information and consolidating member opinion outside of the committee system. While a few junior Republicans disagreed, the vast majority of members interviewed, Democrat and Republican alike, voiced at least general support for the specialization norm. Greg Laughlin (R-TX), a four-term Republican who switched from the Democratic Party to the Republican Party midway through the first session of the 104th Congress, argues that members specialize in areas that will promote their constituency interests.

> For the most part, you [specialize] in those things, one, we're interested in and two, those reflective of our district. The Sierra Club got at me one time. Wait. It wasn't Sierra Club, it was Greenpeace, . . . because I specialize in working for the petrochemical industry. I pled guilty. . . . I only have about 13 or 14 petrochemical companies in my district. Hell, my own brother has worked for one for 25 years. How dumb do they expect members of Congress to be?

Other moderately senior members did not focus on the constituency benefits as much as the institutional benefits derived from specialization. Others extended this to include personal benefits, including power, prestige, and constituency recognition. Representative Myers neglected to discuss the advantages of specialization as much as the disadvantages of not specializing. "Government is very complicated," Myers explains, "It covers so many different areas. And, some people try what I call 'the shotgun approach,' and try to be an expert in every field."

Interestingly, the very senior members were less enthusiastic about specialization. They argue that the need to specialize decreases when a member becomes a subcommittee or committee chair. Two former committee chairmen and one subcommittee chair made reference to the broad jurisdiction of their requisite committees and subcommittees. Former Chair of Appropriations, David Obey explains that junior members should specialize, but, since he is a member of each subcommittee, he must grasp a wide range of issues.

> Well, you specialize the most early on. When I first came here I focused on foreclosing. I focused on corporate farming—things that had import to

my district. I started focusing on occupational health and safety issues because of my personal experience in that field, having worked with asbestos when the bastards who made it knew it caused cancer, but they did it anyway. As I rose in seniority and had more responsibilities, you focus in those areas of responsibility.... And now that I'm ranking member and last chairman of this committee, I have to be more familiar with items in every subcommittee because I belong to each subcommittee.

Former International Relations Chair Lee Hamilton agreed. "It is good to master a subject," Hamilton says, "but you don't need to specialize as much as a committee chair because of [the committee's] broad jurisdiction." Dan Burton, a subcommittee chair and potential committee chair, is also a generalist out of circumstance.

I'm in line to be chairman of the Government Reform and Oversight Committee. That is a very broad committee. I mean, it takes in Washington, D.C. It takes in the Post Office. It takes in all government investigations. It takes in all regulations. I mean, that's probably the broadest based committee in Congress. So, on that committee, you have to be a jack of all trades and a master of as many as possible. In that regard, I try to broaden my horizons.

Based on many of the member comments, specialization's importance appears closely related to a member's efforts to address constituency concerns and further his or her own personal or policy interests. In general, the interviews suggest that most members view committee and subcommittee assignments, coupled with constituency concerns, as the defining factor in the formation of individual specialization.

While a few junior Republicans are content to be generalists, a majority of members interviewed see specialization as an important feature of legislative work. Interestingly, while junior members mention the importance influencing their fellow members, they are somewhat reluctant to link this influence to their committee and subcommittee specialization.

In addition, the interviews appear to illustrate an interesting continuum of opinions concerning specialization. Freshmen and junior members seem less enamored with specialization, although they are attracted to the benefits that specialization can provide. Moderately senior members are unequivocal in their assessment that specialization is an essential feature of committee work because it gives them influence among their colleagues. Committee and subcommittee chairs, however, argue specialization diminishes in importance as they ascend to committee leadership positions. This distribution of the opinions could be a function of the interview sample, or it may illustrate a relationship between a member's length of service and the necessity to specialize. Senior members, committee chairs, and party leaders may not need to specialize anymore because they have attained a position of influence beyond their specialization.

RECIPROCITY

Reciprocity is the natural outgrowth of the specialization norm (Hinckley 1988). In fact, the reciprocity norm subsumes many of specialization's benefits as they relate to a member's influence over his or her fellow members. A House member, through years of committee and subcommittee experience, gains a reputation as an expert in a given area of congressional activity. The member is then sought out by other members when relevant legislation is under consideration. This inevitably leads to spoken or unspoken deference between members corresponding to a given area of expertise. Barbara Hinckley argues that "whether the implementation of the norm involves the trading of votes, bargaining for favors, or tacitly agreeing not to disrupt another member's legislation" depends on the accommodation of a given member (Ibid., 110). In a given situation, members with disparate political views may accommodate each other's specialization and/or constituency interests in an effort to secure a positive relationship. Other members of like political philosophy may accommodate one another through the trading of votes or exaggerated deference.

The reciprocity norm also illustrates the influence of committee and subcommittee chairs in the policy-making process. Several of the more prominent House committees have subcommittees which formulate legislation on a wide array of subjects. Hence, the members of these subcommittees become specialized in these somewhat obscure aspects of public policy. Consequently, when a piece of legislation emerges from a subcommittee, the other members of the committee generally defer to the knowledge and expertise of the subcommittee members (Hinckley 1988; Smith and Deering 1997). Thus, subcommittee chairs, possessing powers similar in scope to those of full committee chairs, can greatly influence the nature and direction of a specific policy arena.

The practice of exaggerated deference extends to the committee level as well. Members without expertise in a given policy area may seek out the committee chair, a senior committee member, or those with similar political philosophies. In fact, Schneier found that chairs and ranking members were 28 percent more likely to offer successful amendments than were non-committee members, suggesting that, in general, a courtesy is extended to more senior, specialized members based on their knowledge and experience (1988). Schneier argues that members see these colleagues as knowledgeable, creating the expertise necessary to trade good will, information, and ultimately votes. Hence, the influence that accrues from member specialization relating to committee and sub-committee experience forms the basis for reciprocity.

As with seniority and specialization, the junior members interviewed were generally less supportive of reciprocity. In this case, junior members argue that trading votes violates the trust between the member and his or her constituency. For example, Sam Brownback is reluctant to coop-erate with other members because he is fearful that he and his colleague may have conflicting motives.

> I get to points where you defer to somebody's knowledge if they know a situation, whether they be a committee chairman or somebody outside that really truly knows the situation, or a member on the other side of the aisle that's been around. You start deferring to their knowledge if they know it better. But, if their knowledge is better but they've been co-opted by the system to the point that they aren't expressing independent judgment, you lose little faith.

Several other members suggest that reciprocity is a necessary evil arising from an incalculable array of policy areas. When necessary, mem-bers are forced by circumstance to rely on the expertise and experience of like-minded colleagues. In some cases, these were state delegation members, members possessing similar ideologies, or trusted friends. For the most part, members were quick to point out that others seek them out as well. In any case, the specialized interests of the member serve to facilitate this exchange. For instance, Mike Oxley finds that his col-leagues can influence his vote through their understanding of certain issues with which he is unfamiliar.

> I don't pretend to have a lot of expertise in some areas, and I clearly rely on [others]. For example, the Intelligence Authorization Bill was on the floor last week. A good friend of mine chairs the committee. I personally voted right down the line with her. First of all, that's a rather arcane area. A lot of that is black. And so you do have to rely on people that have some expertise and you feel are in a general philosophical arrangement with you, and feel the same. I just think that's inevitable and good. It's good for the system. It allows you to develop expertise and allows mem-bers to really delve into these kinds of issues. We need people who are experts in particular areas of the world, on the International Relations

committee. I don't think they get a whole lot of bunk back home for being an expert on Northern Africa. But somebody has to do it. And somebody has to know that stuff, so when you debate foreign aid or debate whatever issue, that you have to rely on their expertise. They've been there, they've studied it, they know the players, all that kind of stuff. Very, very important.

Oxley's suggestion that reciprocal arrangements are "inevitable and good" illustrates his understanding of both the specialization norm and the influence that the specialization norm can provide. It indicates that he relies upon other, more specialized colleagues both for information and guidance. Tim Roemer (D-IN) discusses the other side of reciprocity. Roemer's specialized work on the Education Committee has helped to establish his reputation among his fellow colleagues and secure votes for other legislation.

A piece of education legislation that I developed and modified and drafted through a year, or through a couple year process, and then take that product from the committee to the floor and hopefully get that legislation passed. Other members then think of you in terms of those issues. They associate you with education issues. And that helps you in terms of your ability to get other pieces of legislation passed that don't have relevance to education.

At the other end of the spectrum, Todd Tiahrt (R-KS), a freshman Republican, admits that he also has to rely upon the expertise of his colleagues, especially those senior members from his delegation. Due in no small measure to his familiarity with Pat Roberts' legislative history, Tiahrt defers to his colleague's judgment when a relevant issue arises.

I can give you an example for Kansas. Pat Roberts is the chairman of the Ag. Committee. And, obviously hung around there for a long time, understood how the current system works and had a good plan for reforming it. Well, that's something that I didn't have the time or expertise, even though I grew up on a farm, it's been 25 years since I've had my seat parked in a tractor seat. And so I wasn't real familiar with how to improve the system. And, I deferred my judgment to his, based on his experience, not only in Kansas, but also in Washington, D.C., as a member of the Ag committee and serving as chairman. So, yeah, I think, and on other issues when I vote. There are certain people that I follow.

As previously suggested, committee and subcommittee chairs have an inordinate policy-making influence. Not surprisingly, these members recognize the effect that a member's expertise can have on influencing his

or her colleagues. Some, however, scoff at the notion that they themselves have an extraordinary power due to their position, especially in
light of the recent large independent-minded freshman classes. The hu-
mility, however, of two committee chairs belies the influence the very
senior members possess. Tom Bliley, Chair of the Commerce Committee
consults with numerous members, including those outside of his committee. He is reticent to characterize this exchange however.

> Lots of people contact me as chairman of the committee about issues that
> come up in Congress nowadays. How much deference they give me, that
> I wouldn't want to say. Some may, some may not. I wish more did.

Bliley's comments were echoed by Pat Roberts, Chair of the Agriculture Committee. Like Bliley, Roberts finds that too few freshman members seek his guidance. "I wish they would more. That would be the
idea," Roberts argues. Roberts, however, admits that cooperative arrangements often occur when members lack knowledge in a particular policy
area. in these instances, staff become important facilitators for information exchange. Press Secretary Lisa Gagnon assumes this role in the
Roberts Office. Roberts states that information exchange is the foundation for making good policy decisions.

> I know I do that. When I come to the floor and it's a contentious issue, I
> look immediately to the members who serve on that committee whose
> advice and counsel I trust. And then I go to them and I say, "Now, as I
> understand the argument, or the discussion, or the issue here, it's thus and
> so. You tell me if I'm wrong." And if you have enough of an advance
> period of time, I would tell Lisa to go talk to that staffer in so and so's
> office, because I know that person knows what they're talking about. Then
> you weigh that with what you're hearing from your own district, and if
> there's any kind of a problem there, you've got to figure out why the
> senior member of that committee whose advice and counsel that you trust,
> why they are taking that position. And usually they have a very good
> reason, and you might not know that.

Roberts admits, however, that even a party leader or influential members
may command undue influence.

> I must admit, however, with a wild and woolly question, sometimes it
> doesn't occur that way. You can have somebody standing up at the ear of
> the Speaker, and they can be in charge of damn near anything.

On the whole, it appears that members understand the need for vote trading, information exchange, and general cooperation between members. Once again, junior members were generally less supportive of the congressional norms than were senior members. This may indicate the junior members' lack of true understanding of how the institution operates, or it may suggest that attitudes toward reciprocity are changing and fewer reciprocal relationships will exist in the future. Given the rise of the freshman caucus groups and the importance of reciprocity in that environment, however, this seems unlikely.

The most interesting feature of the reciprocity questions, however, was the members' unwillingness to speak at length about reciprocity. Most of the members interviewed were hesitant to discuss vote trading. In fact, more than one member refused to answer the question, while many appeared uncomfortable and anxious to move on to other topics. A concern about the public perception of this practice may be driving this reaction.

CONCLUDING OBSERVATIONS

In Chapter 4, three current challenges facing congressional norms are analyzed. Further, Chapter 5 discusses the problems arising from party switchers and the effect these have on the seniority system. The discussion of each of these phenomena, however, demonstrates the stability of both the institution and its norms. In fact, it appears that congressional norms can be both stable and resilient. In this chapter, we see why this is the case. Congressional norms are still important because the members believe they are. While junior members generally disagree with seniority, specialization, and reciprocity, they recognize the advantages of each and employ them when possible. Senior members, who are generally supportive of the norms, have worked for years to secure the benefits of committee seniority, policy specialization, and cooperative arrangements. In short, even those members who endorse change, desire institutional stability. Thus, it is easy to see why these norms are so resilient.

These findings suggest some general trends. First, a member's length of service influences his or her appreciation of said norms. Second, junior House members generally oppose the three congressional norms tied to the committee system, while senior members voiced their approval of these same norms. Finally, the most important finding is that norms still matter to the members. While it may be true that norm violations are increasing, as the findings in Chapter 3 suggest, members cite anecdotal

evidence to substantiate the continuing importance of seniority, specialization, and reciprocity.

These anecdotal claims support the overall finding concerning the resiliency of the congressional norms. Periods of reform occasionally occur
in Congress. These periods bring change but rarely instability (Hinckley
1988; Thurber and Davidson 1996). One feature of the institution that
makes it stable is its reliance on informal guidelines, those generally
outside the scope of reformers. Consequently, these norms adapt and
survive despite efforts to the contrary. They provide a degree of predictability peculiar to members governed by the whims of constituents,
interest groups, and party leaders. Thus, this research illustrates why they
survive: norms are important. They are important to the members. They
are important to the institution.

The three challenges to congressional norms discussed in Chapter 4
and the effects of party switchers found in Chapter 5 represent both the
desire for reform and the need for stability. Each of the norms synony-
mous with committee work came under fire directly or indirectly during
the 104th Congress, but only minimal change actually occurred. The
reason that these reform efforts were unsuccessful is that these norms
are still important to the members.

Chapter 7

CONCLUSION AND
SPECULATION

Congressional watchers may view a study of congressional norms as passe. Clearly, the extensive investigatory work of Matthews (1960), Polsby (1971), Fenno (1971), Polsby, Gallaher, and Rundquist (1971), Hinckley (1971), Asher (1973), Matthews and Stimson (1975), Hinckley (1977), Berg (1978), and Stanga and Farnsworth (1978) answered many of the definitional and historical questions concerning the informal rules of Congress. In a sense, these studies provide the foundation for the current understanding of both the formation and purpose of congressional norms. The problem, however, rests not in a greater knowledge of norms in a highly institutionalized Congress, it concerns the general understanding of norms in a more inhospitable environment.

A handful of congressional scholars, including Schneier (1988), Rohde (1988), Smith (1989), Uslaner (1993), Moore and Herrick (1993), Epstien, et al. (1997), have undertaken more recent examinations, during the post reform period. Unfortunately, none of these employ the research method that made many of the earlier studies so informative—they fail to inquire of the members themselves. This study seeks to fill this void in the literature. It does so by asking the members their attitudes regarding three institutional norms during a time of apparent norm instability.

In this examination, there are no casual relationships, instead this study illustrates the numerous questions left unanswered by the past and present research of congressional norms. In that way, this examination differs from current norm analyses in two important ways. First, not since 1975, and Matthews and Stimson's research of specialization, have member attitudes been the primary focus of congressional norm research (1975). Since that time, the U.S. House has witnessed the devolution of institutional comity, the rise of media scrutiny, and two periods of significant reform. Given these changes, an investigation of this sort fills a void in the literature.

Second, this examination includes a factor not previously investigated, namely the institution itself. There exists a gap in the literature between research of the institution's universalistic tendencies (institutionalism) and the promotion of norms that serve to perpetuate these tendencies. The examination of the historical trends in Chapter 3 demonstrates the inherent connection between institutionalism and congressional norms. Congressional norms, especially those promoted by the committee system, thrive in an environment defined by "automatic rather than discretionary methods for conducting internal business" (Polsby 145).

Further, previous research on this subject demonstrates that a universalistic environment flourishes when membership is stable and inclined to advance norms that automate decision making (Price 1971; Kernell 1977; Price 1978). By tracing the evolution of the universalistic House, the relationship between norm compliance and institutionalism becomes apparent, suggesting that an unstable membership is less willing to promote automatic decision-making processes because it limits, even subjugates, their influence.

The effect of the institution in the process of norm relaxation is an important step in a deeper understanding of House norms. Previously, research into norm relaxation has centered on membership change (Weingast 1979; Rohde, et al. 1985) as well as factors not directly related to the institution—environmental factors that might lead to institutional change (Uslaner 1993). Only in an examination of European parliaments have institutional factors been included in the analyses, with striking results (Loewenberg and Mans 1988). The pull of institutionalism on member behavior may also help to explain the continued stability of the institution, given the importance of reelection and influence.

CHANGE VS. STABILITY

The U.S. House is not impervious to change, it just seems that way. In reality, the House undergoes periodic reform with almost every major membership shift. These reforms, however, rarely inalterably change the institution. Instead, they are simply incorporated into the fabric of the institution. In this way, the House tends to gravitate away from the unknown and back to the predictable. This trait maintains institutional stability.

In fact, a quick review of the history of the House illustrates the point. The last reform period to truly change the way the institution functioned was the Cannon Revolt of 1910 (Silbey 1991). Those reforms were the first to empower the individual House member by stripping the Speaker of numerous traditional party and legislative powers, most of which would never formally return to the Speaker. Since 1910, however, three major reform periods—the late 1940s, the early 1970s, and early 1990s—produced some institutional change, but nothing approaching the adoption of individual careerist objectives represented by the Cannon Revolt.

In the case of the 104th House, numerous reforms were adopted. On the surface, many of these may appear to be radical departures from the pre-reform House. The interviews, however, suggest something altogether different. With the exception of the junior Republicans, most of the members maintained that norms threatened by these reforms should be preserved, if for no other reason than abandoning these norms would empower the party or the Speaker. In addition, many members discussed the automatic or predictable nature of norm implementation. For instance, after some 85 years, there is very little about the seniority system that would surprise an experienced House member. A replacement system, however, might bring with it a number of unforeseen outcomes detrimental to the member's career plans. Thus, most members see no need to rock the proverbial boat when doing so might jeopardize their possible position in a future Congress.

This was the prevailing attitude regarding specific changes as well. While junior members and a handful of moderately senior members support the Boehner Rule, a larger group of mostly senior members spoke about need for caution when reforming such an important aspect of members' careers.

Not surprisingly, members tend to speak about norms in terms of their own careers. they were more concerned with how these reforms might affect their position within the institution, instead of the how these reforms might effect the institution as a whole. For instance, regarding the Boehner Rule, junior members use the terms "abuse of power" and "corruption," an obvious reference to their belief that long-time, powerful committee chairs are usurping the power and interests of other, less senior, less powerful members.

As with the junior members, senior members supportive of the Boehner Rule also appear to view the institution from their own particular point of view. Although more likely to discuss institutional change in nonspecific terms, many senior members spoke about the knowledge, experience, and effectiveness they bring to their positions committee and subcommittee chairs.

In short, it appears that a member's service to the institution alters their perception of their role within that institution. Aside from specific legislative goals, junior members perceive that it is their role to change the institution, while senior members are there to prevent the very kind of impetuous change desired by their junior colleagues. Like so many other aspects of the Congress, a balance of sorts has been achieved between immediacy and patience represented by these two groups. Thus, institutional change usually occurs in such a way as to maintain institutional stability.

IMPORTANCE OF CONGRESSIONAL NORMS

Despite the institutional emphasis, the primary focus of this research is the continuing importance of congressional norms. Based on a review of the norm literature, most of which was published prior to the 1970s reforms, one might predict that institutional norms were important to the members. Congressional scholars like Donald Matthews, Nelson Polsby, Barbara Hinckley, and Herbert Asher directly or indirectly argue that norms are important to both House members and the institution.

This research addresses the three congressional norms most closely identified with the committee system: seniority, specialization, and reciprocity. These three were chosen due to their significance in the committee system, another facet of the institution reportedly diminishing in importance. Citing the increase in seniority rule violations, the rise of junior member influence within and outside the committee structure, and the general decay of institutional comity, several scholars argue that the committee-based norms are in rapid and permanent decline (Rohde 1988; Smith 1989; Uslaner 1993; Moore and Herrick 1993; Koopman 1996). While it is true that norms have been relaxed since the highly institutionalized, pre-reform Congresses of the 1950s, congressional scholars may have overstated this decline. Certainly, this research suggests that they have underestimated the continuing importance of norms in the minds of members and the strength of these opinions.

In fact, one of the most striking observations was not just the split of opinions but the strength of those opinions. Members were not nonplussed by the topic, which might have been predicted, given the passage of the Boehner Rule and the literature suggesting the diminishing importance of congressional norms. Instead, most members had what appeared to be deeply held opinions concerning seniority, specialization, and reciprocity. It was also the case that those in support of the norms were just as fervent as those in opposition, something that the literature or prevailing sentiment would not have predicted.

When asking members about the Boehner Rule, the three-year limit on committee chairmanships, junior members were consistently more supportive of chairmanship restrictions than senior members. It was difficult to assess the reasons for these differences however. It could be that junior members witness the advantages of seniority and wish those advantages for themselves. Thus, they support reform measures that might remove the advantages of seniority. It also may be that these members, many of whom ran against the institution, see this as an opportunity to support reforms desired by their constituents. Again, this posits the question of motivation unanswerable at this point.

One of the more interesting findings with regard to the Boehner Rule, however, was the large number of senior Republicans who spoke against it. On the surface, this might not appear unusual considering the advantages of seniority. When one takes into account, however, that on the first day of the 104th House every House Republican voted in favor of the Boehner Rule, this lack of support among senior Republicans may be another illustration of the institution gravitating back to more predictable institutional features.

NORMS AND THE INSTITUTION

Perhaps the most important finding concerns the relationship between the institution and its norms. Given the historical importance of congressional norms, it is surprising that so little work has focused on this aspect of norm research. Clearly, the stability and structure of the institution greatly affect the rule-making and rule-abiding tendencies of its members. The decline in institutionalism, discussed at length in Chapter 3, affects not only the formal rules of the House, but the informal rules as well. Thus, congressional scholars can expect a less institutionalized House will make for a less constrained or civil body.

Uslaner makes the argument that the Congress of the 1990s lacks the civility of previous Congresses (1993). He suggests that this has been an ongoing process, in which the Congress has gradually become an institution where compromise and conciliation have been replaced with distrust and hostility. This is a consequence, he argues, of external forces, namely social incivility, guiding the attitudes and behavior of elected officials. This research demonstrates the possible existence of another important behavioral force. The relaxation of a highly institutionalized House has allowed members to become less civil. In turn, the institution and its members have adopted methods to match these standards. It becomes a chicken and the egg question. Is the institution creating incivility or is it reacting to a greater public incivility?

Clearly, seniority, specialization, and reciprocity flourish during periods of high institutionalization, when a complex, bounded, automatic institution promotes a more hospitable environment for norm adherence. Hence, tracing the rise and decline of institutionalism in the House matches the rise and decline of the norms that rely on a complex, bounded, automatic institution to survive and prosper. These findings illustrate that the generally accepted scholarly argument that the House is far less institutionalized in the 1990s than the pre-reform House necessitates that the restrictive nature of norms be relaxed to mirror this evolution. Thus, a clear relationship exists between the highly institutionalized Congresses of the 1940s and 1950s and close adherence to House norms throughout the period, and the less-highly institutionalized Congresses of the 1980s and 1990s and the relaxation of congressional norms.

McCubbins and Sullivan, building on Polsby's contention that the complexity of the House is determined by internal forces, argue that member turnover is the most important single factor changing the complexity of the institution (1968). The interviews of House members in the 104th Congress takes that one step further by showing that House norms are also tied to the membership turnover, codifying the connection that exists between institutional complexity and the desire for normalizing decision-making mechanisms. Therefore, the stability of rules and membership in the institution affects greatly the predictability of House norms. Based on these findings, a reasonable hypothesis is that congressional norms will continue to remain relaxed until House turnover stabilizes and the current membership gains experience and a desire for institutional stability. In turn, this desire may lead to a rise in norm appreciation. Unless, of course, the 104th freshman class is less career-oriented than previous classes. In which case, they may choose not to adopt the careerist mindset and support a predictable institution.

JUNIOR MEMBERS

One feature of this analysis was the effort to illustrate the additional differences that may exist between generations of legislators. While there is general agreement that a personal and professional ambition exists in all members regardless of tenure (Polsby 1968, Ornstein 1983, Loomis 1988), this research illustrates the clear dichotomy of views concerning methods to fulfill these ambitions. In psychological terms, congressional watchers have only the most general understanding of the way House members conceptualize their career goals. If nothing else, this examination indicates that, if all members have relatively similar career goals, they go about accomplishing these goals in much different ways based on their institutional standing. It may be that junior members conceptualize their institutional standing differently than do their senior counterparts. Thus, the strategies they select to overcome institutional obstacles, for instance seniority requirements, are different than those strategies developed by senior members less affected by these obstacles. Regardless of the specific institutional ambitions, members work toward achieving these ends in different ways. This research not only illustrates these differences but the interview excerpts demonstrate the differing means to achieve these goals.

Specifically, junior legislators consistently spoke against the three norms under investigation. In fact, when discussing the advantages of the Boehner Rule, the junior members were hostile, almost belligerent, toward past committee chairs and senior legislators advocating the continuation of the seniority rule. By disregarding or dismantling the rules that subjugate their influence, junior members can capture powerful positions more quickly. Consequently, when another large group of junior members enters the institution, intuitively one might hypothesize that additional effort to weaken norms will be attempted.

Further, this research illustrates something implied but unsubstantiated in previous congressional research, namely junior members have different attitudes about the institution than their senior counterparts. Three decades ago, Herbert Asher argued that freshmen may *understand* the norms of member interaction, but in asking the same questions, it is apparent that they do not necessary *agree* with them (1973). Hence, members without power and influence are those least likely to favor the system that promotes qualities they do not possess—seniority and expertise.

The implications of these differing attitudes are twofold. First, it further substantiates the long-held belief that membership turnover spawns institutional reform (Rieselbach 1978; Price 1978; Smith 1989; Dodd and Oppenheimer 1993; Rieselbach 1994; Thurber and Davidson 1995; Loomis 1996). Table 4.2 illustrates the relationship between membership turnover and periods of reform. It appears that new members have different attitudes than established legislators and a willingness to advocate institutional reform.

Second, a learning process does occur within the institution, challenging Asher's conclusion that freshmen fully understand institutional norms early in their tenure (1973). Asher interviewed freshman and non-freshman members at one point in time finding that all members have an equal understanding of these norms. The findings here, however, suggest that junior and senior members have different attitudes toward norms, suggesting that these attitudes evolved over their tenure. Obviously, a longitudinal study is needed to fully demonstrate this evolution.

FUTURE RESEARCH

The greatest deficiency of this project is that the results are only a snapshot in time. A gap still exists in the literature regarding the *changing* attitudes toward these norms. Each of the congressional scholars to interview members concerning congressional norms failed to re-interview the members at a later date (Matthews 1960; Asher 1985; Matthews and Stimson 1975; Loomis 1988; and Whiteman 1995). To fully understand the origin of these differing attitudes, one must interview members at several points in their career. At this time, students of Congress cannot fully understand the process by which junior member attitudes evolve into senior member attitudes.

In the future, the 23 House members originally questioned should be re-interviewed to examine how these attitudes change over time. By showing that attitudes evolve as members become more senior, it will provide insight into the groups that advocate reform and their reasons for doing so. Junior and senior members have similar reasons for their differing positions. They both hope to secure institutional benefits. In the case of the senior member, these can best be achieved by supporting congressional norms. The junior member chooses not to support norms for the same reason because institutional norms benefit senior members at the expense of their junior colleagues.

In addition, asking only 23 House members eight questions about three specific norms does not provide the data necessary to determine the existence of statistically significant relationships among and between groups of members. A much larger group of members must be interviewed for any statistical analysis beyond the demonstration of general trends. A natural extension of this project would be to re-interview the original group House members and add another group of members large enough to be able to make statistically justified assertions.

Finally, while congressional scholars may know some things about the attitudes and history of congressional norms in the House, students of

Congress know very little about norms in the Senate. In fact, over the past 40 years, only two scholars have investigated the informal rules of the Senate beyond the descriptive analysis (Matthews 1960; Peabody 1976). Based on these findings, it is argued that House norms and Senate norms are very similar. Some scholars, however, argue that the Senate norms have never been challenged to the degree witnessed in the House (Hinckley 1988; Uslaner 1993; Loomis 1996). In future research, the House research should be duplicated with U.S. Senators and their staff in hopes of determining the attitudinal differences that exist in that institution.

Substantively, this project should have several effects. First, the interviews suggest the existence of previously unresearched or underresearched areas including the existence of an institutional effect on member ability to relax congressional norms. This suggests that the institution itself plays a greater role in member behavior than the current literature suggests. Second, this project should help to once again illustrate the informative nature of interview studies. Since the landmark studies of Matthews, Asher, and Fenno, congressional scholars have become even more enamored with quantitative methods. While regressions can inform research greatly, they are not an end all. In this day and age, few researchers focus on the member as an investigatory tool, when he or she is a wealth of information surprisingly underutilized by scholars.

Finally, the findings should encourage other congressional watchers to re-examine the question of congressional norms. Clearly, norms are not dead. In fact, one might argue they are surprisingly healthy given reform efforts to eliminate them. In any event, norms deserve the attention of congressional scholars, for they assuredly have the attention of the members.

REFERENCES

Alchian, Armen A. 1950. "Uncertainty, Evolution, and Economic Theory." *Journal of Political Economy* 58, no. 3: 211–221.

Aldrich, John H., and David W. Rohde. 1997. "Balance of Power: Republican Party Leadership and the Committee System in the 104th House." Presented at the 1997 Midwest Political Science Association annual convention. Chicago, IL. April 10–13.

Alford, John and David Brady. 1993. "Personal and Partisan Advantages in U.S. Congressional Elections, 1846–1990." In *Congress Reconsidered,* ed. Lawrence Dodd and Brus Oppenheimer. Washington, D.C.: Congressional Quarterly Press.

Asher, Herbert. 1973. "The Learning of Legislative Norms." *American Political Science Review* 67: 499–513.

Bardach, Eugene. 1972. *The Skill Factor in Politics: Repealing the Mental Commitment Laws in California.* Berkeley: The University of California Berkeley Press.

Berg, John. 1978. "The Effects of Seniority Reform on Three House Committees in the 94th Congress." In *Legislative Reform,* ed. Leroy N. Rieselbach. Lexington: Lexington Books.

Birenbaum, Arnold and Edward Sagarin. 1976. *Norms of Human Behavior.* New York: Praeger.

Bolling, Richard W. 1968. *Power in the House: A History of the Leadership of the House of Representatives.* New York: Dutton.

Browning, Robert X. 1997. "Floor Behavior of Freshmen Representatives in the 104th and 105th Congress." Presented at the 1997 American Political Science Association annual convention. Washington, D.C. August 28–31, 1997.

Bullock, Charles S. 1973. "Committee Transfers in the United States House of Representatives." *The Journal of Politics* 35: 85–120.

———. 1978. "Congress in the Sunshine." In *Legislative Reform,* ed. Leroy N. Rieselbach. Lexington: Lexington Books.

Burlington Free Press. May 25, 2001.

Clark, Joseph. 1963. *The Senate Establishment.* New York: Hill and Wang Publishers.

Committee Organization in the House, H. Doc. 94–187, 94th Congress, 1st session, 1975, p. 32. As cited in Davidson and Oleszek. 1994. *Congress and Its Members.* Washington, D.C.: Congressional Quarterly Press.

Congressional Quarterly's Politics in America 1996: The 104th Congress. Washington, D.C.: Congressional Quarterly Press

Congressional Quarterly Weekly Report, assorted dates.

Cook, Timothy. 1989. *Making Laws and Making News: Media Strategies in the U.S. House of Representatives.* Washington, D.C.: Brookings Institution.

Cooper, Joseph. 1970. *The Origins of the Standing Committees and the Development of the Modern House.* Houston: Rice University Studies.

——— and David W. Brady. 1981. "Institutional Context and Leadership Style: The House from Cannon to Rayburn." *American Political Science Review* 75: 988–1006.

Copeland, Gary W. 1987. "Seniority and Committee Transfers: Career Planning in the Contemporary U.S. House of Representatives." *The Journal of Politics* 49: 553–564.

Crowe, Edward W. 1983. "Consensus and Structure in Legislative Norms: Party Discipline in the House of Commons." *The Journal of Politics* 45: 907–931.

Davidson, Roger H. 1992. *The Postreform Congress.* New York: St. Martin's Press.

——— and Walter J. Oleszek. 1994. *Congress and Its Members.* Washington, D.C.: Congressional Quarterly Press.

de Boinville, Barbara, ed. 1982. *Origins and Development of Congress.* Washington, D.C.: Congressional Quarterly Press.

Deering, Christopher J. 1996. "Career Advancement and Subcommittee Chairs in the U.S. House of Representatives: 86th to 103rd Congresses." *American Politics Quarterly* 24: 3–23.

——— and Steven S. Smith. 1997. *Committees in Congress,* 3rd. Washington, D.C.: Congressional Quarterly Press.

Dodd, Lawrence C. 1986. *Congress and Policy Change.* New York: Agathon Press.

———. 1986. "A Theory of Congressional Cycles: Solving the Puzzle of Change." In *Policy Change in Congress,* ed. Gerald C. Wright, Leroy N. Rieselbach, and Lawrence C. Dodd. New York: Agathon Press.

——— and Bruce I. Oppenheimer. 1993. "Maintaining Order in the House: The

Struggle for Institutional Equilibrium." In Lawrence C. Dodd and Bruce I. Oppenheimer, eds. *Congress Reconsidered,* 5th ed. Washington, D.C.: Congressional Quarterly Press.

Epstien, David, David Brady, Sadafumi Kawato, and Sharyn O'Halloran. 1997. "A Comparative Approach to Legislative Organization: Careerism and Seniority in the United States and Japan." *American Journal of Political Science* 41: 965–998.

Evans, Lawrence C. and Walter J. Oleszek. 1997. *Congress Under Fire: Reform and the Republican Majority.* Boston: Houghton Mifflin Company.

Fenno, Richard F. 1965. "The Internal Distribution of Influence: The House." In David B. Truman, ed. *The Congress and America's Future.* Englewood Cliffs, NJ: Prentice Hall.

————. 1971. "The Freshman Congressman: His View of the House." In Nelson W. Polsby, ed. *Congressional Behavior.* New York: Random House.

————. 1973. *Congressmen in Committees.* Boston: Little, Brown Publishers.

————. 1978. *Home Style: House Members in Their Districts.* New York: Harper Collins Publishers.

————. 1989. *Watching Politicians: Essays on Participant Observations.* Berkeley: Institute of Governmental Studies.

Galloway, George B. 1976. *History of the House of Representatives.* New York: Crowell.

Gimpel, James G. 1996. *Fulfilling the Contract: The First 100 Days.* Needham Heights, MA: Allyn and Bacon Press.

Hammond, Susan Webb. 1997. "Congressional Caucuses in the 104th Congress." In *Congress Reconsidered,* 6th ed., ed. Lawrence C. Dodd and Bruce I. Oppenheimer. Washington, D.C.: Congressional Quarterly Press.

Hibbing, John. 1982. "Voluntary Retirement from the U.S. House: The Costs of Congressional Service." *Legislative Studies Quarterly* 7: 57–74.

Hinckley, Barbara. 1971. *The Seniority System in Congress.* Bloomington: Indiana Press.

————. 1977. "Seniority 1975: Old Theories Confront New Facts." *British Journal of Political Science* 6: 383–399.

————. 1988. *Stability and Change in Congress,* 4th ed. New York: Harper and Row Publishers.

Homans, George Caspar. 1962. *Sentiments and Activities.* New York: Macmillan Publishers.

House Republican Conference Rules.

Huitt, Ralph. 1961. "The Democratic Party Leadership in the Senate." *American Political Science Review* 55: 331–344.

Jones, Charles. 1970. *The Minority Party in Congress.* Boston: Little, Brown and Company Publishers.

Jones, Rochelle and Peter Woll. 1979. *The Private World of Congress.* New York: Free Press.

Kernell, Samuel. 1977. "Toward Understanding 19th Century Congressional Careers: Ambition, Competition, and Rotation." *American Journal of Political Science* 21: 49–74.

Kolodny, Robin. 1997. "Republican Party Heterogeneity and Negative Agenda Setting: The Tuesday Lunch Bunch and the Republican Majority in the House of Representatives." Presented at the 1997 American Political Science Association annual convention. Washington, D.C. August 28–31, 1997.

Koopman, Douglas L. 1996. *Hostile Takeover: The House Republican Party, 1980–1995.* Lanham: Rowman & Littlefield Publishers.

Kornberg, Allan. 1964. "The Rules of the Game in the Canadian House of Commons." *The Journal of Politics* 26: 358–380.

Ladd, Everett. 1991. "Like Waiting for Godot: The Uselessness of 'Realignment' for Understanding Change in Contemporary American Politics." *In The End of Realignment? Interpreting American Electoral Eras,* ed. Byron Shafer. Madison: University of Wisconsin Press.

Loewenberg, Gerhard and Thomas C. Mans. 1988. "Legislative Norms in Three Parliaments." *American Journal of Political Science* 32: 155–177.

Loomis, Burdett. 1988. *The American Politician.* New York: Basic Books.

———. 1996. *The Contemporary Congress.* New York: St. Martin's Press.

Manley, John F. 1969. Wilbur Mills: A Study in Congressional Influence. *American Political Science Review* 63: 442–464.

———. 1970. *The Politics of Finance: The House Committee on Ways and Means.* Boston: Little, Brown, and Company.

Mann, Thomas, and Norman J. Ornstein, eds. 1982. *The New Congress,* 3rd ed. Washington, D.C.: American Enterprise Institute Press.

March, James G. and Johan P. Olsen. 1989. *Rediscovering Institutions: The Organizational Basis of Politics.* New York: The Free Press.

Masters, N.A. 1961. "Committee Assignments in the House of Representatives." *American Political Science Review* 55: 345–357.

Matthews, Donald R. 1960. *U.S. Senators and Their World.* New York: Vintage Books.

——— and James A. Stimson. 1975. *Yeas and Nays: Normal Decision-Making in the U.S. House of Representatives.* New York: John Wiley and Sons.

Mayhew, David. 1974. "Congressional Elections: The Case of Vanishing Marginals." *Polity* 6: 295–317.

McCubbins, Mathew D. and Terry Sullivan. 1987. *Congress: Structure and Policy.* London: Cambridge University Press.

Moore, Michael K. and Rebekah Herrick. 1995. "Rethinking Congressional Careers: The Changing Behavioral Implications of Career Path Selection." *Southeastern Political Review* 23: 205–230.

Munger, Michael C. 1988. "Allocation of Desirable Committee Assignments: Extended Queues versus Committee Expansion." *American Journal of Political Science* 32: 317–344.

Niemi, Richard G. and Herbert F. Weisberg. 1993. *Controversies in Voting Behavior,* 3rd ed. Washington, D.C.: Congressional Quarterly Press.

Oleszek, Walter, J. 1996. *Congressional Procedures and the Policy Process,* 4th ed. Washington, D.C.: Congressional Quarterly.

Ornstein, Norman J. 1983. "The Open Congress Meets the President." In *Both Ends of the Avenue,* ed. Thomas Mann and Norman Ornstein. Washington, D.C.: American Enterprise Institute.

———, Thomas E. Mann, and Michael J. Malbin. 1996. *Vital Statistics on Congress 1995–1996.* Washington, D.C.: Congressional Quarterly Inc.

Parker, Glenn R. 1992. *Institutional Change, Discretion, and the Making of the Modern Congress: An Economic Interpretation.* Ann Arbor: University of Michigan Press.

Peabody, Robert. 1976. *Leadership in Congress: Stability, Succession, and Change.* Boston: Little, Brown.

Peters, Ronald M. 1990. *The American Speakership: The Office in Historical Perspective.* Baltimore: Johns Hopkins Press.

Pitney, John J. and William F. Connelly. 1995. "The Speaker: A Republican Perspective." In *The Speaker: Leadership in the U.S. House of Representatives,* ed. Ronald M. Peters. Washington, D.C.: Congressional Quarterly Press.

Polsby, Nelson. 1968. "Institutionalization in the House of Representatives." *American Political Science Review* 62: 144–168.

———. 1971. "Goodbye to the Inner Club." In Nelson Polsby, ed. *Congressional Behavior.* New York: Random House.

———, ed. 1971. *Congressional Behavior.* New York: Random House Publishers.

———. 1983. *Consequences of Party Reform.* Oxford: Oxford University Press.

———, Miriam Gallaher, and Barry Spencer Rundquist. 1971. "The Growth of the Seniority System in the U.S. House of Representatives." In Nelson Polsby, ed. *Congressional Behavior.* New York: Random House.

Porter, H. Owen. 1974. "Legislative Experts and Outsiders: The Two-Step Flow of Communication." *The Journal of Politics* 36: 703–730.

Price, David E. 1978. "The Impact of Reform: The House Commerce Subcommittee on Oversight and Investigations." In LeRoy N. Rieselbach, ed. *Legislative Reform: The Policy Impact.* Lexington: Lexington Books.

Price, H. Douglas. 1971. "The Congressional Career Then and Now." In *Congressional Behavior,* ed. Nelson Polsby. New York: Random House.

Rae, Nicol C., 1994. *Southern Democrats.* New York: Oxford University Press.

Reeves, Andree E. 1993. *Congressional Committee Chairmen. Three Who Made an Evolution.* Lexington: University of Kentucky Press.

Rhode, David W. 1988. *Parties and Leaders in the Postreform House.* Chicago: The University of Chicago Press.

———. 1988. "Studying Congressional Norms: Concepts and Evidence." *Congress and the Presidency* 15: 139–145.

———, Norman J. Ornstein, and Robert L. Peabody. 1985. "Political Change and Legislative Norms in the U.S. Senate, 1957–1974." In Glenn Parker, ed. *Studies of Congress.* Washington, D.C.: Congressional Quarterly Inc.

————— and Kenneth A. Shepsle. 1978. "Thinking about Legislative Reform." In Leroy Rieselbach, ed. *Legislative Reform: The Policy Impact.* Lexington: Lexington Books.

—————. 1987. "Leaders and Followers in the House of Representatives: Reflection's on Woodrow Wilson's 'Congressional Government.'" *Congress and the Presidency* 14: 111–133.

Rieselbach, LeRoy N., ed. 1978. *Legislative Reform: The Policy Impact.* Lexington: Lexington Books, D.C. Heath and Company.

—————. 1994. *Congressional Reform: The Changing Modern Congress.* Washington, D.C.: Congressional Quarterly Press.

—————. 1995. "Congressional Change: Historical Perspectives." In *Remaking Congress: Change and Stability in the 1990s,* ed. James A. Thurber and Roger H. Davidson. Washington, D.C.: Congressional Quarterly Press.

Ripley, Randall B. 1978. *Congress: Process and Policy,* 2nd ed. New York: W.W. Norton and Company.

Roberts, Brian. 1990. "A Dead Senator Tells No Lies: Seniority and the Distribution of Federal Benefits." *American Political Science Review* 34: 31–58.

Schneier, Edward V. 1988. "Norms and Folkways in Congress: How Much Has Actually Changed?" *Congress and the Presidency* 15: 117–138.

Sheppard, B.D. 1985. *Rethinking Congressional Reform: The Reform roots of the Special Interest Congress.* Cambridge: Schenkman Books.

Shepsle, Kenneth A. 1978. *The Giant Jigsaw Puzzle: Democratic Committee Assignments in the modern House.* Chicago: University of Chicago Press.

—————. 1988. "Representation and Governance: The Great Legislative Trade-off." *Political Science Quarterly* 103: 461–483.

Silbey, Joel H. 1991. *The Congress of the United States: Patterns of Recruitment, Leadership, and Internal Structure, 1789–1989.* Brooklyn: Carlson Publishing Inc.

Sinclair, Barbara. 1983. *Majority Leadership in the U.S. House.* Baltimore: Johns Hopkins Press.

—————. 1989. *The Transformation of the U.S. Senate.* Baltimore: Johns Hopkins Press.

—————. 1995. *Legislators, Leaders, and Lawmaking: The U.S. House of Representatives in the Postreform Era.* Baltimore: Johns Hopkins University Press.

Smith, Steven S. 1986. "Revolution in the House: Why Don't We Do It on the Floor?" In Robert L. Peabody and Nelson W. Polsby, eds. *New Perspectives on the House of Representatives,* 4th ed. Baltimore: Johns Hopkins Press.

—————. 1989. *Call to Order: Floor Politics in the House and Senate.* Washington, D.C.: The Brookings Institution.

————— and Christopher J. Deering. 1990. *Committees in Congress,* 2nd ed. Washington, D.C.: Congressional Quarterly Press.

—————. 1997. *Committees in Congress,* 3rd ed. Washington, D.C.: Congressional Quarterly Press.

Stanga, John E. and David N. Farnsworth. 1978. "Seniority and Democratic Reform in the House Representatives: Committees and Subcommittees." In *Legislative Reform,* ed. Leroy N. Rieselbach. Lexington: Lexington Books.

Stewart, Charles III. 1992. "Committee Hierarchies in the Modernizing House, 1875–1947." *American Journal of Political Science* 36: 835–856.

Sundquist, J.L. 1981. *The Decline and Resurgence of Congress.* Washington, D.C.: The Brookings Institution.

Swenson, Peter. 1982. "The Structure of Power in the U.S. House, 1870–1940." *Legislative Studies Quarterly* 7: 225–258.

Thurber, James A. and Roger H. Davidson, ed. 1995. *Remaking Congress: Change and Stability in the 1990s.* Washington, D.C.: Congressional Quarterly Press.

U.S. Senate Document. "Senators Who Changed Parties During Senate Service (Since 1890)."

Uslaner, Eric M. 1993. *The Decline of Comity in Congress.* Ann Arbor: University of Michigan Press.

Weingast, Barry. 1979. "The Rational Choice Perspective on Congressional Norms." *American Journal of Political Science* 23: 245–262.

White, W.S. 1956. *Citadel: The Story of the United States Senate.* New York: Harper and Brothers.

Whiteman, David. 1995. *Communication in Congress: Members, Staff and the Search for Information.* Lawrence: University of Kansas Press.

Wildavsky, Aaron. 1975. "The Past and Future Presidency." *Public Interest,* Fall 1975.

Wilson, Woodrow. 1885. *Congressional Government.* Boston: Houghton Mifflin Publishers.

INDEX

About the Author

JUDD CHOATE is a former assistant professor of political science at the University of Nebraska and faculty fellow at the University of Nebraska Public Policy Center. From 2000 to 2002, he served as director of the Nebraska Minority and Justice Task Force, researching racial and ethnic bias in the Nebraska court system. Dr. Choate has a Ph.D. in political science from Purdue University and is currently attending the University of Colorado School of Law.